God, the World, and Me

A Look at Diverse Views of Scripture from the Bible

From the Perspective of a Psychiatrist

Clemmie Palmer, III, MD

Copyright ©2018 Clemmie Palmer, III, MD

All International Rights Reserved

ISBN 978-0-9861946-7-2 (eBook)

ISBN 978-0-9861946-8-9 (Paperback)

DEDICATION

I am deeply grateful to the faculty of Hood Theological Seminary for the education I received there. In particular, I wish to acknowledge four professors:

To Dr. Trevor Eppehimer
Thank you for introducing me to the wonders of Systematic Theology and for setting the standard of courage and imaginative thinking to which I continue to aspire.

To Dr. Sondra Coleman
I thank you with deep gratitude for the priceless lectures on leadership skills from which I am still reaping many benefits.

To Dr. André Resner
Thank you for introducing me to the concept of authentic worship for which I strive daily.

To Dr. Ken Walden
You always told your students to write to positively impact others. Just wanted you to know that I heard you. Thank you.

Acknowledgments

I would like to thank my wife, Veronica, for her unconditional support. She unselfishly allowed me to divide my time between home, work, and school.

My son, Clemmie IV, and my daughter Angel are the fuel that drives the engine. I want them to know that learning is a lifelong journey and one never gets too old to learn.

Further, my mother, Ms. Martha Mitchell, instilled a work ethic in me that made my education possible.

My brother, Charles, particularly inspired me during my study of C.S. Lewis in Chapter 9.

Finally, Zirenthia Holcombe, my sister and pharmacist, forced me to think critically about topics such as the Trinity and Salvation.

Preface

This book is for the seminarian as well as the layperson who want a quick view on some of the major topics covered in seminary. The emphasis here is on salvation, redemption, sin, apocalyptic literature, as well as the Lord's Supper and its purpose.

It is the goal of this writer to get the reader to think outside the box and understand that a diversity of views can enrich one's own position, and should be encouraged.

Table of Contents

Chapter I: Finding God 1
Endnotes - Chapter 1: Finding God 11
Chapter II: The New Testament.. 13
Endnotes - Chapter II: The New Testament 31
Chapter III: Sin and Evil... 33
Endnotes - Chapter III: Sin and Evil................................. 43
Chapter IV: Revelation 45
Endnotes - Chapter IV: Revelation 63
Chapter V: Relating to God 65
Endnotes - Chapter V: Relating to God 77
Chapter VI: Election 79
Endnotes - Chapter VI: Election 90
Chapter VII: Another View of Redemption...................... 91
Endnotes - Chapter VII: Another View of Redemption . 103
Chapter VIII: Theological Nearsightedness.................... 105
Endnotes - Chapter VIII: Theological Nearsightedness . 114
Chapter IX: Evangelism.. 115
Endnotes - Chapter IX: Evangelism 127
Chapter X: The Lord's Supper.. 129
Endnotes - Chapter X: The Lord's Supper 137
Chapter XI: Homosexuality and the Church................... 139
Endnotes - Chapter XI: Homosexuality & the Church ... 148
Chapter XII: Sermon on Forgiveness 149
Endnotes - Chapter XII: Sermon on Forgiveness 156
A Personal Note from the Author 157
About the Author 158

Chapter I: Finding God

You have heard people say over the years, after they had a life-transforming experience, that they changed because they found God. These types of statements, and the insistence that this is wholeheartedly true, inspired great thought about salvation. For this writer's response to these "I found God" comments, let us go to the book.

God was never lost. God the creator of the world cannot be lost. This leads us to some characteristics of God. Before the characteristics of God are expounded on, it is important to look at a few scriptures in Colossians to emphasize that man was lost (dead in sin) and had to be found.

Two different Bible versions will be used here. For the record, this writer understands the benefits of studying several different biblical translations, thinking it is nearsighted to only rely on one translation for knowledge.

"When you were dead in your sins and in the uncircumcision of your flesh, God made you alive with Christ. He forgave us all our sins, having canceled the charge of our legal indebtedness, which stood against us and condemned us; he has taken it away, nailing it to the cross. And having disarmed the powers and authorities, he made a public spectacle of them, triumphing over them by the cross" (NIV Col. 2:13-15). These scriptures are foundational to this writer's theology.

Another view from the Message Bible will perhaps shed additional light on this matter since different translations affect readers in different ways.

"When you were stuck in your old sin-dead life, you were incapable of responding to God. God brought you alive- right along with Christ! Think of it! All sins are forgiven, the slate wiped clean, that old arrest warrant canceled and nailed to the cross. He stripped all the spiritual tyrants in the universe of their sham authority at the Cross and marched them naked through the streets." The point here is that God found mankind dead in sin. God was never lost, but man is lost unless man is made alive in Christ.

The next logical question is, "How does man get connected to Christ since man is dead before being alive in Christ?" For this answer let us turn to the influence of John Wesley.

Salvation begins with God. John Wesley, the father of Methodism, taught, and this writer concurs, that mankind has a choice in their salvific way. However, the Calvinist believes that unconditional election is the gist of salvation. Salvation is initiated, cultivated and is consummated by God.

According to John Wesley there is a synergistic relationship between God and man. In other words, one plus one equals two $(1 + 1 = 2)$. Relationally, synergism looks like this. If a man wants to date a lady, then he should ask her. She has to say yes then and only then, he can take her on a date. An agreement has been made. The man cannot take her on a date without her consent. This will be kidnapping, an unjust act.

God will not kidnap anyone and force a relationship with them. The Bible states "… His work is perfect, and all His ways are just…" (Deut. 32:4). According to John Wesley, all theology must center on the salvation of man. Humankind is saved by God's free grace. Wesley's belief can be correlated to Isaiah 55:1 (KJV): "Ho, every one who thirsts, come ye to the waters, and he who has no money; come ye, buy, and eat; yea, come, buy wine and milk without money and without price."

Water is a metaphor for the enjoyment of our salvation. Wine and milk are symbols of complete satisfaction. The only way to achieve complete satisfaction is to work out our own salvation. God must act first. Mankind loves God because God loved man first.

Salvation begins with prevenient grace to all, as recorded in Wesley's sermon, "On Working Out Our Own Salvation." This is a type of grace whereby God softly whispers to man and brings man under conviction. Man must respond to this prevenient grace by first., allowing God's energy to work within us. The acceptance of prevenient grace leads to remorse and, more importantly, repentance.

Next, a justifying or saving grace comes into being. This is the moment Jesus is accepted as our Savior and Lord with complete confidence that he died and was resurrected for the sins of man on an individual basis. This entails a belief that man is free from sin and the guilt of sin. According to Wesley, salvation begins the moment we are justified. Sin, a dis-ease, is cured by God's grace.

The last type of grace is perfecting grace. Perfecting grace means that man grows in faith and grace, according to Wesley. This is the type of grace that leads to Christian perfection as expanded upon in Wesley's sermon "Christian Perfection." Christian perfection is a "never ending aspiration for all of love's fullness" or "grace abounding."

On the other hand, the Calvinist position is monergistic, which means that God is the only player in this process. There is no relationship. Mathematically, it is described as one plus zero equals one (1+ 0 = 1). This one does not represent a true partnership. This is rather odd, relationally.

Next, this writer will contrast the Calvinist view with the Arminian view of salvation.

In the eighteenth century, predestination was held in high esteem by the Calvinist and opposed by the Arminians. In short, John Wesley, an Arminian, believed that predestination made God the author of sin. Calvinism was summarized at the council of Dort in Holland in 1618 with the acronym, TULIP.

T represents total depravity. In other words, man has no ability to save himself. John Wesley was a proponent of depravity but not teetotal depravity. Man was made in the image of God and everything God made he deemed good. "So God created humankind in his image, in the image of God he created them…" (Gen. 1:27).

According to Wesley, man was created in a state of original righteousness. There will always be a part of the creator imprinted on his human creation. Human behavior is independent of this divine imprint upon humankind. Wesley refers to this imprint as the image of God.

God created in man a free will. This is the ability to exercise a liberty of choice. Liberty requires that every man should have trials. God gave man a free will and according to Romans 1:18-20, a mind of understanding to assist this free will. Man made a choice to reject God, the Creator, and changed his own image of the perfect God into one of defilement. Man's decision did not change God's image and did not (because behavior could not) erase the divine imprint on him. Nevertheless, man became unrighteous. There were consequences after the fall of man, which included bondage to the devil, a dis-ease state, and a dis-tempered nature.

A renewal of man to his original state means that God graciously initiated (by asking for a date as in the example above) this renewal and has therefore saved mankind through his son, Jesus the Christ. Without this renewal, there would not be any hope to receive salvation first from the "dawning of grace in the soul till it is consummated in glory." How is all this possible?

Father God, through his grace and mercy, incarnated his son, Jesus, who paid the price (atonement) for man's sin on the cross. Jesus' life, death, and resurrection saved Man. Father God now sees man through the righteousness of Jesus and, therefore, man is restored to the original image of God. Jesus's righteousness was imputed to man.

2 Corinthians 5:21 (NLT) says it best: "For God made Christ, who never sinned, to be the offering for our sin, so that we could be made right with God through Christ."

U, in the TULIP acronym, stands for unconditional election. The Calvinist teaches that one is elected not based on what they do or the type of life lived. The Arminian position is that of universal election.

L in TULIP is for limited atonement. This is the Calvinistic belief that Jesus died only for the elect. Jesus died for all, according to John Wesley and the gospel of John: "For God so loved the world that he gave his only Son, so that everyone who believes in him may not perish but may have eternal life" (John 3:16).

Next is the I and P in the acronym TULIP. According to Calvinists, the I stands for irresistible grace. Arminians believed that preparing grace is resistible. This means that God, in his sovereignty, dispenses his drawing grace or calling (which would bring man to salvation if responded to with faith) in such a way that man can reject it. Therefore, it is stated that the Arminian position is synergistic. This is the doctrine that the human will cooperates with the Holy Spirit in the work of regeneration. An example of this doctrine is, "If I love you and you love me back, then we have a relationship."

P represents perseverance of the saints. The common parlance for this is "you can't lose your salvation" or "once saved, always saved." In other words, one cannot backslide. In short, Wesley believed, and this writer concurs, that man can backslide like David with Bathsheba.

Now this writer will focus more specifically on the meaning and the way to salvation with a house metaphor.

Wesley wrote in *The Scriptural Way of Salvation* that "… Salvation is the entire work of God, from the first dawning of grace in the soul till it is consummate in glory." One is immediately saved from the penalty of sin (pardon follows repentance when one believes that Jesus died on the cross for their sin), progressively from the plague of sin (perfecting grace, witness of the spirit, and gradual development of holy living), and eschatologically from the very presence of sin and its degenerative effects. The great end of religion is to renew our hearts in the image of God, to repair that total loss of righteousness and true holiness, which we sustained by the sin of our first parent.

Salvation is initiated in the yard by God's prevenient grace. If responded to in the affirmative, by faith, then one moves to the porch of salvation where repentance occurs. Repentance opens the door of salvation.

The door is called the "threshold" almost or midway in the house.[3] One can go in the house or turn around. This grace is known as justifying or forgiving grace. One is justified by faith. One is given a pardon, which is a forgiveness of sin. The past is clean. The sole condition is imputed faith by God through prevenient grace.

Next, there are several rooms in the house, which over time have to be inspected and corrected by God. This work of God is known as perfecting grace (Christian perfection, sanctification). Wesley's doctrine is that Christian perfection is a "never ending aspiration for all of love's fullness" or "grace abounding." Perfect love is sanctification. Salvation is the cure to the diseased state of sin.

One can have all the head knowledge and still be unsettled in their assurance of salvation.[4]

According to Wesley, one has to have a testimony of the Spirit, "an inward impression of the soul, whereby the Spirit of God immediately and directly witness to my spirit that I am a child of God, that Jesus Christ has loved me, and given himself for me; that all my sins are blotted out and that I, even I, am reconciled to God." One cannot have a steady pace, nor avoid perplexing doubts and fears with the testimony of the Spirit, but once one receives the Spirit of adoption, the peace that passeth understanding will keep us on course, pressing on the upward way, new heights to gain every day with perfecting grace.

How does one grow in grace? One grows in grace through the means of grace. Repetition of the means of grace cannot be an end in themselves, but toward an end, which is a closer walk with God and becoming a mature Christian. The means of grace help Christians overcome our tempers (emotions) that seduce us into deeds, words, and thoughts that make our Christian walk become "broken cisterns that hold no water" (Jer. 2:13).

Means of grace aid the Holy Spirit in two ways: (1) by being a strong inhibition to backsliding, and (2) enhancing growth in grace. The means of grace are as follows: searching the scriptures so that the words of scripture become the word of God, prayer, Lord's Supper, spiritual conversation, attendance at public worship, using the church year as a guide to disciplined spiritual growth, accountability, and acts of mercy and deeds of kindness.

The goal of every Christian should be to go on to perfection. If this is not the goal, then what should a Christian go on to? This striving keeps one from being a Pharisee. If one does not have a goal, one will feel that they have arrived. The Apostle Paul wrote, "Therefore let us go on toward perfection, leaving behind the basic teaching about Christ, and not laying again the foundation: repentance from the dead works and faith toward God, instructions about baptisms, laying on of hands, the resurrection of the dead, and eternal judgment" (Heb. 6:1-2).

Christians claiming perfection are not free from infirmities of both body and mind. Christians cannot expect to be free from temptation. In what sense then are Christians perfect?

Christians should strive to cease from an outward act (or from outward transgression of the law). Christians should be holy in all manner of conversation and free from harboring evil thoughts. Christians should be free from holding grudges and nourishing temptations. Perfecting grace affirms that justification delivers us from the guilt of our sins; perfect love gradually delivers us from the power of sin over us. We all need to grow in grace.

Salvation begins with Genesis 1:27. Therefore, I am not defined by my behavior. I am only described by my behavior. Unlearning can be very difficult. For example, I was always taught that man was born in total depravity, which has been vehemently contradicted by John Wesley. Moreover, Jesus has to be my savior (my "personal savior," not an intellectual trip) before he can be the Lord of my life.

Let us look at Jesus in the New Testament as foundational to believe in a personal savior.

Endnotes - Chapter 1: Finding God

1. Roger E. Olson, The Story of Christian Theology: Twenty Centuries of Tradition and Reform (Downers Grove, IL: IVP Academic, 1999), 459.
2. Albert C. Outler, John Wesley's Sermons: An Anthology, ed. Albert C. Outler & Richard P. Heitzenrater (Nashville: Abingdon Press, 1991), 372.
3. Donald W. Haynes, On the Threshold of Grace (Dallas: TX: UMR Communications, Inc., 2011), 72.
4. Randy L. Maddox, Responsible Grace: John Wesley's Practical Theology (Nashville, TN: Kingwood Books, 1994), 124.

Clemmie Palmer, III, MD

Chapter II: The New Testament

The New Testament, in particular the Gospels and the book of Revelation, is a source of comfort for some and a source of uncertainty for others. Let me explain.

The New Testament is the foundation of the church. These twenty-seven books have influenced Western culture immensely. This influence has been social, political, personal, and religious. The Gospels will be expanded upon to highlight their role in the New Testament. A literary-historical approach will be utilized by this writer. The perspective of the ancient historian is emphasized. The goal is to determine, as much as possible, what the Gospels meant to the early Christians.

All of the New Testament books were originally written in Greek. Most scholars agree that they all were written more or less between 50 AD to about 120 AD. Historically, it is believed that Jesus was born around 4 BC and died about 30 AD. There are a few complicating factors in regard to the Gospels which are:

1. The Gospels are all post-resurrection writings about Jesus
2. Jesus spoke Aramaic and Greek is the language of the New Testament
3. Some of the original manuscripts have been redacted
4. Authorship of the Gospels is unknown
5. The author of the Fourth Gospel is dialectical in approach, and

6. No writings of Jesus (if he wrote any) have been found.

The Gospels are attributed to Jesus' disciples (followers) or to others who had an association with the disciples. Matthew and John were disciples. Mark had an association with Peter, and Luke was a companion of the Apostle Paul.[1]

The word apostle means, "One who is sent." Paul was "grandfathered" into this family of apostles after his Damascus experience and historically at the Council of Jerusalem when Peter, James, and John gave him the right hand of fellowship. (Galatians 2:7-10)

The Gospels are the only books in the Bible that describe Jesus' birth, life, death, and resurrection. Therefore, the books are the beginnings of Christianity. The gospels make up the first of four categories of the New Testament. The second category of the New Testament is the book of Acts. Acts centers on the spread of Christianity. The third category of the New Testament includes twenty-one Epistles. These letters were written to communities or individuals to teach them what to believe and how to govern their behavior. The last category of the New Testament is the book of Revelation. Revelation points to God's eternal kingdom in which he makes all things new.

One needs to be acquainted with the Jewish context in which these books were written to properly understand and appreciate the Gospels. God chose Israel as his people. "For you are a people holy to the Lord your God; the Lord your God has chosen you out of all the people on earth to be his people, his treasured possession" (Deut. 7:6).

A covenant was made with Abraham, the patriarch, before the covenant at Mount Sinai regarding descendants and land. In *Paul Was Not a Christian: The Original Message of a Misunderstood Apostle,* Dr. Eisenbaum, author and professor, highlighted the belief that the Abrahamic covenant provided assurance to the Israelites of their everlasting relationship with God. According to Dr. Eisenbaum, the law was a gracious gift that reinforced their special status as God's people.[2]

Blessings and curses were associated with the legal, the familial, and the special relationship between God and his people. Punishment was viewed by the Israelites as a sign of wholehearted commitment on behalf of God, since they are his saved people. Ancient Israelites, for the most part, were not following the law for salvific purposes. They were keeping the law out of a commitment to the intimate relationship they had with God.[3]

"The Fourth Gospel is the only Gospel claiming direct eyewitness origins, most scholars assume it is primarily theological rather than historical in its character."[4] Karl Bretschneider, biblical scholar, argued that a reasonable scholar must choose between the Synoptic Gospels (Matthew, Mark, and Luke) and John. Given this three-versus-one ratio the Synoptic Gospels win.[5] However, Matthew, Mark, and Luke are called the Synoptic Gospels because they can be placed side by side in columns and viewed together although they are not without incongruences.[6]

For example, Matthew and Luke write two different birth narratives. Mark does not write a birth narrative. Moreover, a rich man (Mark Chapter 10) asks Jesus, what must he do to inherit eternal life. Only in Matthew is he described as young (19:20) and only in Luke is he described as a ruler (18:18). Nevertheless, since the Synoptic Gospels are similar to one another in ways they are different from John-- proximity to Jesus, historical setting, and theological meaning--these controversies make it difficult to imagine scholarly consensus about a book, also called the "Enigmatic Gospel," the "Maverick Gospel," and the "Spiritual Gospel" in contrast to the Synoptic Gospels.[7]

It is the belief of the writer of this book that there are four Gospels and that each one should be uniquely viewed from its own perspective to achieve a more complete picture of Jesus. A comparison of the Synoptic Gospels will follow, culminating in the Fourth Gospel.

The Gospel of Mark was the first Gospel written. John Mark is the attributed author of this book. This author was an educated Greek-speaking Christian who wrote about thirty-five to forty years after the life of Jesus. The first verse of Mark gives the reader a clue to the type of writing this gospel is: "the beginning of the gospel of Jesus Christ, the Son of God" (Mark 1:1).

Gospel means good news. Mark was not writing a historical document but was trying to convey a message that he inherited from oral tradition. The message was that Jesus was the unrecognized messiah who had to suffer and die.

The term Christ is Greek and means anointed. The Hebrew meaning of Christ is the word messiah. First century Jews were expecting a great cosmic figure or at least a great military leader like King David to overthrow the Roman government and the forces of evil. Jesus was killed by the Roman government.

After Jesus is announced by John the Baptist, a Jewish prophet, he performed many miracles. For the most part, he was not recognized. In fact, some thought he was possessed by the Beelzebub (Mark 3:22), his family thought he was mentally ill (Mark 3:21), and he was not believed by people in his hometown (Mark: 1-6). Interestingly, in the Gospel of Mark only God and the demons knew fully who Jesus was.

After Jesus was baptized "... a voice came out of Heaven stated, 'You are My beloved Son, in You I am well-pleased'" (Mark 1:11). The Gerasene demoniac ran to Jesus... "bowed down and shouted, 'What business do we have with each other Jesus, Son of the Most High God? I implore You by God, do not torment me'" (Mark 5:6-7).

A miracle that is found only in Mark occurs when Jesus heals the blind man in Bethsaida. Jesus, after the second attempt, healed this man (Mark 8:22-26). In the next story,

Jesus asked his disciples "who do people say that I am?" Peter correctly answered the Messiah (Mark 8:29).

After this Jesus told his disciples that he must suffer and be killed, and after three days rise again. Peter in verse 30 rebuked Jesus for these statements. Immediately after this, Jesus rebuked Peter. The disciples did not understand that Jesus had to suffer and die to be the Messiah.

Even Jesus seems to question his situation. He prays three times for God to remove the cup from him in Gethsemane (Mark 14:32-42). Then he cried out in a loud voice, "My God, My God, Why Have You Forsaken Me?" (Mark 15:34).

The veil of the temple was torn from top to bottom after Jesus' death. This would have resonated with the Jewish people. The veil separated the Holy of Holies from the rest of the temple. It is the room, it is believed, that God dwelled. After Jesus' death, according to Mark, God became directly accessible to his people.

The other books that make up the Synoptic Gospels are Matthew and Luke. Most scholars agree that both Matthew and Luke used the book of Mark as a source for their writing. Matthew and Luke have a number of stories in common with Mark, which includes but is not limited to: the Gerasene demonic healed, Jairus' daughter healed, the man with a withered hand healed. Matthew and Luke also have a number of stories in common that are not found in Mark, which includes but is not limited to: the Lord's Prayer, the

Beatitudes, and the healing of the centurion's servant. Most scholars agree that the material which is found in Matthew and Luke but not in Mark came from a hypothetical source, called Q, which no longer survives.[8] Q is derived from the German word quelle which means source.

Scholars believe that Matthew and Luke had their own individual sources, M and L respectively, for stories that are unique to them. For example, the healing of the two blindmen is only in Matthew, Chapter 9:27-31 and the widow's son raised from the dead is only in Luke, Chapter 7: 11-17.

The Gospel of Matthew has been attributed to Matthew. He was a disciple of Jesus, known to be a tax collector. Matthew was a Greek-speaking Christian who wrote this gospel around 80-85 AD. In the very first verse of Matthew, the writer traces Jesus' genealogy back to Abraham. "The record of the genealogy of Jesus the Messiah, the son of David, the son of Abraham" (Matthew 1:1). Matthew's readers, and certainly first century Jews, believe that Abraham was thought to be the father of the Jewish people.[9]

The events in Matthew regarding Jesus seem to unfold according to a divine plan--the virgin birth, an angel went to Joseph in a dream to convince him to wed Mary, and their flight from Egypt. On several occasions, Matthew uses a label called a "fulfillment citation" which linked the present event to a prophet. These fulfillment citations are unique to Matthew. Matthew showed that Jesus was the long-expected Messiah of the Jews. In short, Jesus was the Jewish Messiah, sent by the Jewish God to the Jewish people in fulfillment of the Jewish scriptures, according to Professor Bart Ehrman at the University of North Carolina at Chapel Hill.[10]

The final book of the Synoptic Gospels is Luke. Jesus is described as a Jewish prophet who was rejected by the Jewish people, and therefore Jesus' message of salvation was proclaimed to all people, Jews and Gentiles.

Traditionally, this gospel is attributed to a Gentile physician named Luke and was written in Greek between 80-85 AD. Luke provides a genealogy of Jesus just like Matthew, albeit quite different. Luke's genealogy of Jesus is traced back to Adam, the progenitor of the human race. Unlike Matthew, where the emphasis was on Jesus' connection to Abraham, the father of the Jewish people, Jesus is connected to Adam the father of humanity.

Therefore, through Jesus, salvation comes to all. Jesus preaches like a prophet, heals like a prophet, and dies like a prophet. The story whereby Jesus raised a widow's son (who was not an Israelite) from the dead in Nain (Luke 7:11-17) echoes the prophet Elijah's raising of the dead son of a widow in Zarephath (1 Kings 17:7-24). Luke portrays the crowd recognizing that Jesus was a prophet, "… and they began glorifying God, saying, 'A great prophet has risen among us!' and, 'God has visited His people" (Luke 7:16).

Jesus dies like a prophet. This claim is only in Luke. "Nevertheless I must journey on today and tomorrow and the next day; for it cannot be that a prophet would perish outside of Jerusalem" (Luke 13:33). Since Jesus is a prophet and knows God's will, he is calm and at peace before his death. Jesus even has an intelligent conversation with one of the criminals on the cross, which led to this criminal's salvation. No agony is displayed. In comparison, Mark's picture is one of agony.

Lastly, Luke had a more social agenda than the other writers of the Gospels. It may be because Luke knew that the Gospels needed time to spread to the world, allowing the Gentiles time to repent. Therefore, in Luke, Jesus was highly concerned about those who were poor, hungry, and thirsty.

The author of the book of John is anonymous. The author of this gospel is called the beloved disciple. Some argue that this beloved disciple was: John, son of Zebedee, Thomas, Lazareth, and Mary Magdalene among others. Others argue that the author of the Fourth Gospel was John (not the son of Zebedee) who identified himself as the Elder in second and third John.

Another group of scholars proposed that the author was an apostolic witness to Jesus. This theory is important since it can explain some of the difference between the book of John and the Synoptic Gospels. This book will attribute the author of the Fourth Gospel to the traditional author, John, son of Zebedee, although the evidence is not vast. The book was written between 90-100 AD.

There are distinctive features of John which include: first, the introduction is presented in the form of a community worship confession, "and the Word became flesh and lived among us, and we have seen his glory, the glory as of a father's only son, full of grace and truth" (John 1:14), and the presentation of signs (instead of miracles).[11] There is no secret in the Gospel of John. In Mark Chapter four, it is asked, "who is it that the wind obeys." In John, the reader knows who is performing the signs. The miracles are performed in the Synoptic Gospels in response to a person's faith.

In the Fourth Gospel, signs are performed to generate faith. In Mark Chapter 5, Jesus raised Jairus' daughter from the dead. Jairus states to Jesus, "My little daughter is at a point of death. Come and lay hands on her, so that she may be made well and live." At the house there was a commotion. Jesus put them all outside except for the deceased girl's parents and those who were with him. Jesus took the girl by the hand and said, "Talitha cum" which means "little girl, get up!" Immediately the girl got up and began to walk about. Jesus told them that no one should know and told them to give the girl something to eat.

This story is contrasted to the raising of Lazarus from the dead in John Chapter 11. After Jesus had heard that Lazarus was ill, he stayed two days longer in the place where he was. Jesus told his disciples that Lazarus was dead. Jesus stated, "for your sake I am glad I was not there, so that you may believe."

Lazarus had been dead four days at the time Jesus arrived at his tomb. Jesus stated, "Father, I thank you for having heard me. I knew that you always hear me, but I have said this for the sake of the crowd standing here, so that they may believe that you sent me." "When he had said this, he cried in a loud voice, 'Lazarus come out!' The dead man came out…and Jesus said to them, 'unbind him, and let him go'" (John 11:1-44).

Another important difference between the Synoptic Gospels and the Fourth gospel is the way Jesus taught. In the Synoptic Gospels, Jesus taught about the Kingdom of God through parables and brief responses. Jesus never told a parable in the Fourth Gospel. Jesus never tells his disciples of his divine identity, as opposed to the Fourth where his divinity is front and center. Jesus is focused on God and the Kingdom of God in the Synoptic Gospels. In contrast, the Fourth Gospel emphasized Jesus' divinity and his salvific significance.

Why is the Fourth Gospel regarded as different by many scholars as compared to the Synoptic Gospels? Many of the stories that are well known in the Synoptic Gospels are absent in the Fourth Gospel; Jesus' birth narrative, his baptism by John the Baptist, his institution of the Lord's Supper, and his casting out of demons.

This gospel was thought to have been written after the Synoptic Gospels because of its high Christology. The logic is that it took time for this theological development to occur. On the other hand, the writings discovered at Qumran in 1947 revealed a teaching similar to the Fourth Gospel. Since the writing at Qumran predates the Christian movement, one cannot solely explain the differences between the Synoptic gospels and the Fourth Gospel based on the later date of John's composition. The Logos metaphor suggests a Greek mode of thought and thus a Hellenistic worldview influence in the Fourth Gospel.

Moreover, the Fourth Gospel uses a particular form of self-disclosure called the "I am" disclosure. "These speeches employ a pronouncement formula regularly in hymns or aretalogies of gods and heroes in Greco-Roman tradition."[12]

The story about the woman caught in adultery was not in the original manuscript of the Fourth Gospel. This points to more than one author. One should not read the book of John with assumptions in mind which contribute to the apparent dichotomy between the Synoptic Gospels and the Fourth Gospel. "No longer can we read the Synoptic Gospels as straight forward, history. They are all written 'on the slant.' Nor can we assume that John's Gospel, merely because it departs so radically from the Synoptic Gospels, is less reliable historically."[13] As a matter of fact, it is more probable that the passion narrative in John presents a more historical account of Jesus' last days compared to the Synoptic Gospels. Another characteristic of John (other than its seemingly more accurate passion narrative) is its unique style.

The Fourth Gospel is a book of tension. This may be because of the author's dialectical approach. "Dialectical - thinking represents an advance form of reflection in which issues are considered from more than one perspective. While there is truth in one aspect of an issue, other sides of that issue also ring true and a dialectical approach holds truths together in tension."[14]

This dialectical style of the Fourth Gospel, maybe the main reason why some readers have difficulty accepting this gospel at the same level in which the Synoptic Gospels are accepted.

Most readers, at least unconsciously, want to be told, "A leads to B and B leads to C." However, John gives the reader characteristics of "A and B" which invites the reader to make their own conclusion regarding "C." Despite an emphasis on Jesus' divinity in the Fourth Gospel as compared to the Synoptic Gospels, Jesus' humanity is also presented with supporting material.

On the one hand, Jesus' divinity is mentioned in the beginning of this gospel. "… and we have seen his glory, the glory as of a father's only son…" (John 1:14). Further, "Jesus (turned water into wine) did this, the first of his signs, in Cana of Galilee, and revealed his glory; and his disciples believed in him" (John 2:11).

Jesus called God his Father, thereby making himself equal to God (John 5: 17-18). On the other hand, Jesus' humanity is also presented: "and the word became flesh and lived among us…" (John 1:14). Jesus' human family is referenced as son of Joseph (John 1:45), and "… one of the soldiers pierced his side with a spear, and at once blood and water came out" (John 19:34).

The Fourth Gospel has many differences as well as similarities to the Synoptic Gospels as written earlier. John, the presumed author, had his own agenda which was to present another view of Jesus other than the human view of the Synoptic Gospels.

John emphasized Jesus' divinity as compared to the Synoptic Gospels but gave equal weight to Jesus' humanity in the book itself. This portrayal gives readers a well-rounded view of Jesus. Jesus, in the Fourth Gospel, is an agent of God (and God himself) who in him is salvation for all people. Jesus does signs to prove himself to be true.

One must understand first century thinking and culture to ascertain why it was difficult for some people to accept Jesus, although he showed signs to demonstrate who he was during his walk on earth. The Jewish people were looking for peace, not persecution.

Revelation is an apocalyptic book written by John of Patmos around 94-95 CE close to the end of the reign of Domitian, an egoistic Roman emperor. Domitian issued an imperial order for him to be addressed as Lord and God. All subjects were to worship him as the chief God. Revelation through John of Patmos confronts this persecution, this Roman rule and the imperial cult associated with it. Revelation emerged from persecution.

Therefore, the intended readers are the ones who were suffering at the time. John writes a message of hope as revealed to him by Jesus. The apocalyptic story is from

God's perspective. Revelation is not a futuristic book to be viewed in a linear manner on a timeline as explained by the Irish Anglican priest, John Nelson Darby and his followers.

The apocalyptic genre was used by the Hellenistic Jews and early Christians to give meaning to a world of evil, injustice, suffering and the transcendent Heaven itself. Many factors influence this genre of literature, which includes but is not limited to ancient sources like the I Enoch, the Dead Sea Scrolls, the Torah, "Deuteronomistic History," Persian influence during captivity, and the Hebrew prophets, which will be elucidated in detail later.

Many people today hear the word apocalypse and think major disaster or the end of time. However, John of Patmos used it to mean disclosure. The original Greek word is apokalypsis; when translated into English is revelation. Revelation means to reveal or to disclose as of something not yet realized.

Apocalyptic writing was at its heyday from 250 BCE through 200 CE. There is no generally accepted definition by biblical scholars for this type of art but there are several categories, which attempt to explain it:

1. a body of literature,
2. a world view where there is no separation between the religious and the secular, and
3. a specific group within a society.

Although there are no commonly accepted definitions by scholars, there are some common characteristics that crystallize this kind of writing. Apocalyptic literature is dualistic (good versus evil, rich versus poor) in ideology. The existence of man is viewed as worldly as well as cosmic in scope. There are bad things going on in Heaven and on earth.

According to Professor Stephen Cook, in *The Apocalyptic Literature*, "Apocalyptic literature frequently imagines Heaven and earth as separate realms of existence, which parallel and mirror each other. Transcendent molds, or archetypes, in Heaven often prefigure and orchestrate the course of history on earth. Supernatural entities in Heaven frequently invade earth to achieve divine goals."[15]

Another important characteristic of this literature is that the world is evil in some way. There is conflict behind the scene of what is visible of a supernatural nature (God and Satan) at work among people and institutions according to Dr. Bruce Metzger at Princeton Theological Seminary.[16]

The most comforting property of this art is a belief that God is coming soon. A new world will come soon. This new world will be as in the beginning without persecution, idolatry, and anything that is not God centered. The Ancient world pictured a new world in the context of a sinusoidal wave whereby they (the Israelites) had committed wrongs as defined by the Torah and they were oppressed because of sin. The oppression is the valley of the sinusoidal wave.

Then the Lord would give them judges who delivered them from their enemy's hands. This new freedom is the peak of the wave. This peak represented a new world. However, whenever the judge died, they would relapse and behave worse than their ancestors, following other gods, worshiping them and bowing down to them (Judges 2:19). This created another valley and the cycle repeated itself.

The ancient people believe that God created the world and man sinless; God punishes sin against him, and that God gives second chances. These beliefs are exemplified in four stories in Genesis: Adam and Eve's decision, Cain's murder of his brother, world wickedness leading to the great flood, and the arrogance at Babel.

Additionally, the Hebrew people thought that someone must be in control. God created the earth from chaos. It was a formless void and darkness covered the face of the deep. The habitants were created during the first three days of creation. On day one, God created light. The sky and dry land with vegetation was created on day two and three respectively. The inhabitants were created during days four through six. The sun, moon, and stars were created on day four and the fish and fowl on day five. Animals and man, the last of God's creation, was created on day six, then God rested on the seventh day.

God saw everything that he had made, and indeed, it was very good (Genesis 1:31). The way the world was created represented order, structure, and purpose. For the

Hebrew people, the one in control must be God, since God is represented by order, structure, and purpose.

Endnotes - Chapter II: The New Testament

1. Harry Gamble, The New Testament Canon: Its Making and Meaning (Eugene, Oregon: Wipf and Stock Publishers, 2002), 68.
2. Pamela Eisenbaum, Paul Was Not A Christian: The Original Message of a Misunderstood Apostle (New York, New York: HarperCollins, 2009), 82.
3. Pamela Eisenbaum, Paul Was Not A Christian: The Original Message of a Misunderstood Apostle (New York, New York: HarperCollins, 2009), 88.
4. Paul Anderson, The Riddles of the Fourth Gospel: An Introduction to John (Minneapolis, Minnesota: Fortress Press, 2011), 2.
5. Paul Anderson, The Riddles of the Fourth Gospel: An Introduction to John (Minneapolis, Minnesota: Fortress Press, 2011), 105.
6. Bart Ehrmam, The New Testament: A Historical Introduction to The Early Christian Writings (New York, New York: Oxford University Press, 2012), 106.
7. Paul Anderson, The Riddles of the Fourth Gospel: An Introduction to John (Minneapolis, Minnesota: Fortress Press, 2011), 2.
8. L. Michael White, Scripting Jesus: The Gospels in Rewrite (New York, New York: HarperCollins, 2010), 428-429.
9. Bart Ehrmam, The New Testament: A Historical Introduction to The Early Christian Writings (New York, New York: Oxford University Press, 2012), 115-116.

10. Bart Ehrmam, The New Testament: A Historical Introduction to The Early Christian Writings (New York, New York: Oxford University Press, 2012), 132.
11. Paul Anderson, The Riddles of the Fourth Gospel: An Introduction to John (Minneapolis, Minnesota: Fortress Press, 2011), 12.
12. L. Michael White, Scripting Jesus: The Gospels in Rewrite (New York, New York: HarperCollins, 2010), 351.
13. Carl Holladay, A Critical Introduction to the New Testament: Interpreting the Message and Meaning of Jesus Christ (Nashville, Tennessee: Abingdon Press, 2005), 201.
14. Paul Anderson, The Riddles of the Fourth Gospel: An Introduction to John (Minneapolis, Minnesota: Fortress Press, 2011), 129.
15. Stephen Cook, The Apocalyptic Literature (Nashville, Abingdon Press, 2003), 24.
16. Bruce Metzger, Breaking the Code: Understanding the Book of Revelation (Nashville, Abingdon Press, 1993), 18.

Chapter III: Sin and Evil

The ancient world did not envision a world of evil created by God. If God created evil through man, it would be God's fault vicariously. Certainly, God did not create evil. Everything was deemed good in the beginning per God's own words and represented order, structure, and purpose. Hence, a dualistic view developed, good versus evil. Apocalyptic literature emphasizes this dichotomy and forces the reader to take a side. There is no middle ground. The question to be answered by the Hebrew people is, how did evil enter the world if God is not in the equation? One possible answer lies in the book of I Enoch.

Enoch was the father of Methuselah and the grandfather of Noah. What Enoch had to say was extremely important in the ancient world. "Enoch walked with God; then he was no more, because God took him" (Genesis 5:24). I Enoch is a collection of writings that were composed between the late fourth century and the beginning of the Common Era around 100 CE.

Caution: the reader should not necessarily believe that Enoch wrote I Enoch since the ancient people were known to write a piece of work and put someone else's name on it. Part of I Enoch was found with the Dead Sea Scrolls. Parts are derived from images of the Old Testament. This work provides the foundation upon which other writings are based.

Parts of I Enoch are seemingly contradictory. However, this is not unusual in apocalyptic or other Biblical writings. For example, did it rain forty days or one-hundred and fifty days during the great flood of Noah's time?

The authors of apocalyptic literature in the Ancient world did not always make qualifying adjustments to their writing. They would put two traditions in the same story, which may in some instances, cause confusion. Nevertheless, the book plays a role in apocalyptic literature.

Evil had to come from somewhere. According to I Enoch, there were entities in Heaven other than God. These entities are heavenly beings. The ancient people believe that they (the ancient people) were the center of the universe. The movements of the heavenly bodies indicated that these bodies were alive. Actually, the Earth was moving. Angels were in Heaven already in primordial time.

Some of these angels saw the beautiful women and came to earth to have sex with them. These women delivered children that were called Nephilim, giants who were evil destructive beings. God was displeased because heavenly beings were not supposed to sleep with humans. God appeared to humanity with his heavenly host. God placed judgment on the angels as well as the human beings. The human beings perpetuated the evil by being tempted and giving in to the temptation. In this case, God is pictured on a mountaintop directing the battle.

The chief rebel angel, Shemihazah, knew the act of sex with the daughters of men was wrong. The rebel angels broadcasted their desire for earthly women and a goal to beget children by them. Shemihazah replied, "I fear that you will not want to do this deed, and I alone shall be guilty of a great sin."[1]

For these angels' (watchers') sin was identified initially not as immoral. It was identified as revealing hidden heavenly secrets mainly related to metal, mining, magic, and manipulating things. These teachings led to violence and promiscuity. Asael, a rebel angel, taught all the iniquity on the earth and revealed the external mysteries that were in Heaven. Now, sin is changed to a forbidden mixture of flesh and spirit. Immorality has appeared. Enoch saw the judgment place of God and the watchers were annihilated but they did not die. Their spirit will plague earth until the final judgment.

Enoch describes three major eras of the world through dream visions. The first era is from the creation of the world to the flood. This flood represented universal judgment. Other judgments were very specific, for example against Adam and Eve and against Cain. Humans got a demotion and were depicted as animals. Angels were described as fallen stars. All humans were seen as cattle.

The first star to fall was Aseal. Other stars fell from Heaven. As stars fell, they became bulls and mated with heifers, which produced camels, elephants, and asses. The first era ends with God's judgment in the flood.

The second era is the renewal of creation after the flood. Humans are still animals. Noah is a white bull. White symbolizes victory. Noah had three sons. Ham and Japheth were represented by red and black bulls respectively. Shem was pictured as a white bull. Shem's bloodline led to Abraham, Isaac, and Jacob. Jacob was depicted as a white sheep. Jacob was the father of Israel. This sheep is described as the blind going astray by unbelief and apostasy.

These sheep will be victims of wild beasts, the Gentiles, who punish Israel for their apostasy, just as Jacob was punished by his brothers for bragging about his coat. The punishment of Israel was always believed to be deserved in their eyes. This leads to judgment. Seventy angelic shepherds were sent to maintain the sheep until the end times arise. Some shepherds did not maintain their post and became evil shepherds. This dream ends with a theophany. There was a three-fold judgment: against the rebel angels, disobedient shepherds, and the apostate sheep.

The third era begins after the final judgment is over. The author presents a picture that is partly displayed in Revelation. God constructs a New Jerusalem. The Gentiles pay homage to the Jews. The Jews of the diaspora returns. The dead are raised. Finally, the great white bull is born.

All beasts and birds are transformed unto God's likeness. The end times return to the beginning. In this new time of creation, Jews and Gentiles will not be different. Israel's oppression, secondary to the hands of the gentiles, will end. No more red or black bulls. The kingdom of God has been born. This is an encouraging message to a people who do not know where to turn. The only place to turn is to a supernatural one. The Lord will come because he represents order, structure and purpose.

A discussion of the Hebrew prophets is necessary for apocalyptic literature. This literature was heavily influenced by the Torah, Deuteronomistic history, and the prophets. The prophets were chosen by God to be his official representative. These men spoke for God himself. God communicated his message to the prophets through several means, which included but were not limited to dreams, visions, miracles, voices and nature.

The prophets' lives were often endangered because of God's message and God's message was often rejected. There are several themes in these writings which are the sins committed by God's people, the call to repentance, and the warning of the judgment for their sins.

Sin is defined as social injustice, reliance on other nations, false religion (the worship of idols and other gods), and the breaking of the covenant made in Exodus. People were suffering through no fault of their own which is not the formula of "Deuteronomistic history" which is summarized as if the Israelites keep God's commands, they will be blessed and if they do not they will be cursed (Deut. Chapter 28).

The prophet, Amos, addressed Israel during the days of King Uzziah of Judah and in the days of King Jeroboam II.

The Israelites were very religious people. They went regularly to shrines for worship, had festivals, and offered sacrifices to the Lord. The poor were being oppressed simultaneously as the Israelites practiced their religion. "Thus says the Lord: For three transgressions of Israel, and for four, I will not revoke the punishment; because they sell the righteous for silver and the needy for a pair of sandals- they who trample on the head of the poor into the dust of the earth, and push the afflicted out of the way; ... they lay themselves down beside every altar on garments taken in pledge; and in the house of their God they drink wine bought with fines they imposed" (Amos 2: 6-8).

Micah was also concerned with social justice and the poor. The Lord through Micah asked, "Can I tolerate wicked scales and a bag of dishonest weights" (Micah 6:11)? The Lord required the Israelites to do justice, to love kindness, and to walk humbly (Micah 6:8).

The Israelites forgot their commitment to the Torah. "Hear the word of the Lord, O people of Israel; for the Lord has an indictment against the inhabitants of the land. There is no faithfulness or loyalty, and no knowledge of God in the land. Swearing, lying, and murder, and stealing and adultery break out; bloodshed follows bloodshed ... My people are destroyed for lack of knowledge; because you have rejected knowledge, I reject you from being a priest to me. And since you have forgotten the law of your God, I will also forget your children" (Hosea 4: 1-6).

Jeremiah reiterated God's covenant and God's command. "For the day that I brought your ancestors out of Egypt, I did not speak to them or command them concerning burnt offering and sacrifices. But this command I gave them, 'Obey my voice, and I will be your God, and you shall be my people; and walk only in the way that I command you, so that it may be well with you'" (Jeremiah 7:22-23). The Lord did not condone idol worship. He wanted his people to be a holy people.

The Lord was crushed by Israel's wanton heart that turned away from him, and their wanton eyes that turned after their idols (Ezekiel 6:9). What is in their mind shall never happen--the thought, "Let us be like the nations, like the tribes of the countries, and worship wood and stone" (Ezekiel 20:32). The Israelites turned their backs to God and not their faces. In a time of their trouble, they said save us. The Lord replied, "but where are your gods that you made for yourself" (Jeremiah 2:27-28)?

Jeremiah prophesized captivity for the Israelites because of their sin. "I am going to bring upon you a nation from far away, O house of Israel… But in those days, I will not make a full end of you. And when your people say, 'Why has the Lord our God done all these things to us?' you shall say to them, 'As you have forsaken me and served foreign gods in your land, so you shall serve strangers in a land this is not yours'" (Jeremiah 5:15-19).

Jeremiah wrote that the Israelites he was speaking to were worse than their ancestors. "It is because your ancestors have forsaken me, says the Lord, and have gone after other gods and served and worshipped them, and have forsaken me and have not kept my law; because you have behaved worse than your ancestors, for here you are, every one of you, following your stubborn evil will, refusing to listen to me. Therefore, I will hurl you out of this land into a land that neither you nor your ancestors have known, and there you shall serve other gods day and night, for I will show you no favor" (Jeremiah 16:10-13).

Hosea referred to idol worship as adultery. Israel is the bride of Yahweh. "My people consult a piece of wood, and their divining rod gives them oracles. For a spirit of whoredom has led them astray, and they have played the whore, forsaking their God. They sacrifice on top of mountains, and make offerings upon the hills. Under oak, poplar, and terebinth, because their shade is good. Therefore, your daughters play the whore, and your daughters-in-law commit adultery" (Hosea 4:12-13).

Yahweh was not only jealous of other gods and idols; the Lord was jealous of other nations. Yahweh did not want his people relying on other nations. God would have redeemed Ephraim (Israel) if they had repented. This is another example of the God of second chances as supported by four stories in Genesis (Adam, Cain, Noah, and babel).

"Ephraim has become like a dove, silly and without sense; they call upon Egypt, they go to Assyria. As they go, I will cast my net over them; I will bring them down like birds of the air; I will discipline them according to the report made to their assembly. Woe to them, for they have strayed from me! Destruction to them, for they have rebelled against me! I would redeem them, but they speak lies against me" (Hosea 7:11-13).

These prophets give the reader the essence of what was going on in the Hebrew world prior to the fall of the Southern Kingdom to Babylon in 586 BCE. This is what John of Patmos did. He wrote about what was going on in his world for the people of his time to persuade them to maintain the courage and keep the faith because the Lord would return soon.

In addition to the prophets, New Testament writers also wrote apocalyptically. This is exemplified in Mark Chapter 13. It is the consensus among New Testament scholars that Mark 13 was not the work of the historical Jesus. This body of work was an interpretation of Jesus' theology.

The Roman-Jewish war was from 66-70 CE and Mark was written between 75-80 CE within ten years of the destruction of the temple in Jerusalem. Characteristically of apocalyptic literature, it had a pessimistic view of the current world history and anticipated an end to the current situation either by God or God's representative. Jesus spoke of three deceptive warnings to his disciples. He warned them that there would be deceivers, they would undergo persecution themselves, and that they would see the desolating sacrilege.

Now just to correlate Bible history with world history, in 167 BCE Antiochus Epiphanes, a Syrian ruler, decided to impose more Greek culture (Hellenization) on the Jewish people by converting the Jewish temple into a pagan sanctuary and requiring Jews to sacrifice to the pagan gods.[2] This led to the Maccabean revolt and independence for the Jews in Palestine until 63 BCE when the Roman general, Pompey, conquered it.

The appearance of the abomination of desolation, first described by Daniel, signals the onset of persecution. Mark 13 had three major points; first, the Son of Man was coming; second, they were to be watchful of the Lord's glorious second coming and a concluding address for all to "keep awake." The gist here is that the end is coming, and no one knows except God the Father.

This brings us to the book of Revelation.

Endnotes - Chapter III: Sin and Evil

1. George Nickelsburg and James Vanderkam, 1 Enoch: A New Translation (Minneapolis, Fortress Press, 2004), 23.
2. Bart Ehrman, The New Testament: A Historical Introduction to The Early Christian Writings (New York, Oxford University Press, 2012), 56-57.

Clemmie Palmer, III, MD

Chapter IV: Revelation

By 63 BCE in the Roman providence of Asia, Asia Minor, most of the people were Christians. However, there were still some Jews and Jewish-Christians in that area also. There were major persecutions of the Christians at the hands of Rome. Before one can truly understand Revelation, it is of utmost importance for the reader to first understand some basic rules to help navigate through Revelation.

Apocalyptic writings have several characteristics that one must know to understand Revelation. Visions, beasts, numbers, and colors are throughout Revelation and their significance should not be minimized. Excerpts from an interpretive guide, written by Dr. Robert McLawthorn of Hood Theological Seminary are used to assist students as they study about symbolic visions.

"Symbolic visions are not descriptions of things but descriptions of symbols of things. The person 'seeing' the vision begins by assuming that a persecution is in progress, and concludes with a symbolic description of the end of that persecution and a description of a new age with the persecution removed.

The visions come in a series; not in chronological order, but usually the same vision (or a parallel vision) repeated several times, each time becoming more intensified and powerful in nature. The person seeing the vision does not understand the symbolic images that are shown. There is always a heavenly interpreter or mediator (usually an angel) present who explains the meaning of the visionary scene. In Christian apocalyptic literature, Christ himself is often the interpreter.

There are standard symbols in apocalyptic literature. Beasts are one such symbol. Beasts in almost all cases represent nations. The heads and horns of the beasts are usually representative of rulers of particular nations. It is important to understand that the rulers being represented depend on the events at the time of the writing. Any description of future events pertains to the immediate future and portrays the new age that is coming.

Dr. James Efird, professor of Biblical interpretation at Duke Divinity School, believes that numbers and their multiples have specific meanings. The meanings of these numbers must be applied consistently.
The meaning of the numbers does not change and include the following:

1. Three is the realm of the spirit,
2. Four represents created order,
3. Seven represents completeness or appropriate fulfillment,
4. Ten suggests completeness with the idea of total inclusiveness,
5. Twelve represents the people of God, and
6. Three and one-half "always used to symbolize the length of time that evil is allowed to run its course, persecuting the people of God."[1]

Multiples of the numbers are often used to emphasize what is being described. However, the original meaning of the number does not change. Numbers are not to be taken literally but they are to be understood by their meaning.

Colors are also important as one studies Revelation as described by Dr. Efird. White is the most common color in apocalyptic writing and symbolizes victory. Red is indicative of war or conflict. Black indicates a lack of something; for example, a lack of food in a famine. Greenish-gray or pale is the color of a corpse and represents death.[2]

These colors were combined with numbers and beasts to deliver a message to the audience at one point in history. Some of the original meanings have been lost through the years. One has to make an educated guess and speculate on what the writer was saying. Additionally, one should not conclude that there is a hidden meaning behind every work. In psychoanalytic circles, a popular phrase was coined by Dr. Sigmund Freud and may make this point clear, "sometimes a cigar is just a cigar."

With this background in mind, the purpose of Revelation will be explored. Only those who remain faithful under persecution will be inducted into the kingdom of God. There was some negativity regarding Christians in the early second century because of the way they worshiped, among other factors. For example, the Eucharist led non-Christians to believe that Christians were cannibals. Historical sources document persecution of the Christians.

"The first-blown persecution appears to have been under Nero. According to Roman historian Tacitus, Nero made a public display of Christians, having them clothed in animal skins to be eaten by ravenous dogs and others rolled in pitch and set aflame to light his public gardens."[3]

Nero condemned Christians for arson although they were innocent. Nero used Christians as scapegoats for burning Rome. Additionally, in 112 CE, Pliny, the governor of Bithynia-Pontus in Asia Minor, wrote a letter to Emperor Trajan documenting the arrest of Christians and his execution of some of them if they did not prove their loyalty to the state. It was not a crime in Rome to be a Christian; however, it was a crime to refuse to worship the state God.

Trajan, in a written reply, gave approval to Pliny's treatment of Christians, except that Christians were not to be actively pursued and he forbade anonymous accusations that someone was a Christian.

Revelation 1:1-2 (NRSV) "The revelation of Jesus Christ, which God gave him to show his servants what must soon take place; he made it known by sending his angel to his servant John, who testified to the word of God and to the testimony of Jesus Christ, even to all that he saw." Soon is in the first verse of Revelation and is characteristic of the apocalyptic thought. John of Patmos expressed God in the first Chapter and others as the one "who is and who was and who is to come."

God is identified as Alpha and the Omega (Rev. 1:8) which is another way of saying God's created order and the history of the world are under his domain.

John of Patmos wrote to the seven churches of Asia Minor. Each individual letter was meant for all of the churches. Nevertheless, each church had specific characteristics, which were addressed in the letters. John was in the spirit on the Lord's Day, he was instructed by a loud voice to write to the seven churches, to Ephesus, Smyrna, Pergamum, Thyatira, Sardis, Philadelphia, and to Laodicea. John saw seven golden lampstands (the seven churches) and in their midst he saw one like the Son of Man, clothed with a robe and with a golden sash across his chest (royal emblem of a king). His hair was white (victory) as snow and his eyes were like a flame of fire (indication of judgment), his feet like burnished bronze, refined in a furnace (conflict), and his voice was like the sound of many waters.

In his right hand he held seven stars (which are the Angels of the seven churches), and from his mouth came a sharp, two-edged sword, and his face was like the sun shining with full force. Jesus said that he was dead but is alive forever and ever and that he has the keys to Death and of Hades. This defeat of death by Jesus meant to the Christians in Asia Minor that it was Jesus not Caesar who determines who lives or dies.

It is not clear why John addresses the seven letters to the angels of the churches other than he was instructed to do so by Jesus. Ancient people took guardian Angels as literally true. It may have been that John was given these visions and he was supposed to share with the guardian angels and the people were to hear these messages vicariously. Another possibility is that the Angels (messengers) are the leaders of the church or ones who believe the message taught by the church. Apocalyptically, writing to a guardian Angel would be the same as writing directly to the church.

The church at Ephesus was charged with abandoning the love they had at first. They did not have sensitivity anymore and were without mercy to others. To everyone who conquers by repenting and keeping the faith, they will be given permission to eat from the tree of life that is the paradise of God.

There was no chastisement of the church of Smyrna. The church of Smyrna was told that they would suffer ten days of affliction by the devil.

The second death is first mentioned in Revelation. It is to be feared. This church members considered themselves poor, but Jesus declared that they were rich. They were promised the crown of life if they were faithful until death. Moreover, the first death was not to be dreaded since it is not an eternal separation of man from God.[4]

Pergamum prided itself as one of the emperor's favorite cities. It was the center of the cult of Rome. It is described as Satan's throne in Revelation 2:13. The whole church of Pergamum was chastised because some held to the teachings of Balaam (which is symbolic of all false teachings) and to the teaching of the Nicolaitans, a Gnostic group.

Gnostics believe that the world was divided into two spheres, one being spiritual which was good and pure, the other sphere was the material world, which was evil. A spark of the spirit was trapped in every man by matter, the body. A selected few somehow learned the deep secrets of the spirit and their spirit can be reunited with the pure spirit at death.

There were two extreme groups of Gnostics. One group concentrated more on the physical. They chose to punish the body by whipping themselves so that blood could be released thereby exposing the entrapped spirit. The other group believed that they could do whatever they wanted if the spirit was not involved. This rationale led to orgies. (For completeness, some Gnostics outside of the above referenced groups lived an ascetic lifestyle.)

The church at Pergamum was told if they did not repent that the Son of Man would make war against them with his mouth. Further, to everyone who conquers will be given the hidden manna and a white stone upon which a new name is written that no one knows except the Son of Man and the one who receives it. This white (victory) stone seems to represent a ticket for admission to a certain group like it did in the ancient world. This new name is indicative of who really has the real power. It is God, not the emperor.

The letter to Thyatira is the longest of the seven letters although it is the smallest of the seven cities. The Son of Man knew their works. They exhibited love, service, and patient endurance. The whole church was chastised for tolerating the woman Jezebel. It is not known whether this is the woman's real name or Jezebel could be used symbolically as the woman who married King Ahab of Israel who led him to worship Baal (Kings 16:31-33).

The influence of Jezebel was to practice fornication and to eat food sacrifice to idols. Sexual imagery is also used for idolatry. The Son of Man said that he is throwing Jezebel on a bed (because he gave her time to repent and she did not) and all who commit adultery with her will be thrown into great distress unless they repent. The ones who repent and the ones who hold fast and continue to do his work will be given the morning star. Jesus Christ is the morning star, the reward in the cosmic struggle between good and evil. The victory is already won by Christ who will pass it on to those who conquer.

Sardis was the worst church since they were dead with a name of being alive. This church was in a slumber. However, a few did not soil their clothes. The ones who awakened out of their slumber and the ones whose clothes were not soiled, names will not be blotted out of the book of life. The book of life gave the reader assurance during their time of persecution. This figurative book of life also told the reader who was in charge and was encouraging those undergoing persecution.

The Son of Man is described to the church of Philadelphia as the Holy One, the True One, the One who has the key of David who opens doors no one can shut. This was the best church that kept the Son of Man's word and never denied his name.

The church of Philadelphia dealt successfully in their opposition to those of the synagogues of Satan (those groups that were against the Christians). They will be kept from the hour of trial that was coming to the whole world to test the inhabitants of the earth. The church was told to hold fast to what they have, so that no one may seize their crown. If they conquer, they will be made pillars in the temple of God. Further, Jesus would write on them the name of God, the name of God's city, the new Jerusalem, and his own name. The writing of their names by Jesus is a matter of understanding by this steadfast church rather than control.

Laodicea was the last of the seven letters because it was the last church on the road from Ephesus. This was a lukewarm church in a wealthy city known for textile manufacturing, banking, and medicine, particularly eye salve. Water had to be piped into this city from a hot spring. Therefore, when the water arrived in the city it was lukewarm.

John of Patmos considered this historical fact when he described the church of Laodicea. (Again, John was writing for the people of his day.) They thought they were rich, but they were really poor, blind, and naked. Jesus still loved this church. "Listen! I am standing at the door, knocking; if you hear my voice and open the door, I will come in and eat with you, and you with me" (Rev. 3:20). The one who conquers will be given a place on Jesus' throne. The essence of the letters is that one must remain faithful. One needs to see oneself as God sees them.

John had a unique vision of God, according to the book of Revelation. While John was still in the spirit, he saw God's throne room. In Chapter 4, all of creation worships God. The Jewish people believe that creation was divided into four categories: the wild beast (lion), the domesticated animal (ox), humans (face like a human), and birds (eagle). God is in control of creation. They are around his thrown giving praise. The throne room is an imperial designation. Words like legal, royal, etc. were transferred to God.

This would have resonated with the Christians in Asia Minor. For example, the heavenly throne room, which is God's, and the contrasting earthly throne room, which is the emperor's. The heavenly throne room is the center of the universe ruled by God. The phrase "you are worthy" (in verse 4:11) to God is also a way to greet the Roman emperor when he entered a city. Twenty-four thrones were around God's throne and on these thrones, were twenty-four elders. This maybe another political reference. When the emperor held court, 24 officials set in a semicircle around his throne with fasces, which symbolized their authority. (Note that 24 is a multiple of 12.)

Chapter 5 of Revelation is central to the theology of the Christian church. John sees a scroll in the right hand of God, the Father. The contents of the scroll are not made known. The contents of the scroll may be, given the context of Revelation, God's final judgment of the persecutors of God's people at the time Revelation was written. The inference here would be that God's mind was made up.

The scroll was written on the front and the back. It was sealed with seven seals. Wills and testaments were usually sealed with seven seals. Seals and signet rings were an extension of the person who wrote them. No one was worthy (in Heaven, on earth, or under the earth) to open the scroll except the Lion of the tribe of Judah, the root of David because he represented value here, not necessarily power or strength.

These two phrases, Lion of the tribe of Judah, and the root of David would remind the reader of the expectations of the Messiah in the Old Testament, and the great warrior, David, who drove out or killed all of Israel's enemies.

Another goal of the Messiah would be to gather all of the dispersed Hebrews to the promised land. Jesus has already been in battle and won. This is documented by "the Lion of the tribe of Judah, the root of David, has conquered, so that he can open the scroll and its seven seals" (Rev. 5:5).

The seer saw between the throne of God and the four living creatures and among the elders a Lamb standing as if it had been slaughtered, having seven horns and seven eyes. These seven horns represent complete power and the seven eyes are symbolic for complete wisdom. This power and wisdom are manifested on earth through the seven spirits (Holy Spirit).

The lamb took the scroll from the right hand of God who was seated on the throne. Subsequently, all of creation worshiped the Lamb. We are told in this chapter that death is not the end; the one who conquers death lives again.

The cycle of the seven seals follows the Lamb taking the scroll in Revelation Chapter 5. John of Patmos has a series of visions. In the visions, humanity and creation suffer. The language gets more and more eccentric. Beyond these points the seals, trumpets, and bowl judgments are saying the same thing. Chapter 6 begins with a series of three (spiritual) cycles of seven (denoting which has come to maturity). These cycles are not arranged in a linear fashion. They signify that persecution was becoming more difficult to handle.

After the lamb begins to open the seals, the judgment of the world begins in Chapters 6 through 11 and 16 through 18. The first cycle of seven seals is located in Chapters 6 and 7. The seals are followed are by a second cycle of seven trumpets in Chapters eight through eleven. An interlude occurs in the seventh chapter whereby 144,000 (a multiple of 12 and 10) where the people who remain faithful to God and were not apostate were sealed. This elite category did not protect them from persecution or from being martyred.

Next is the third cycle of seven bowls in Chapters 16 through 18. The three in the number of cycles is spiritual and is not historical. The two documented ways of understanding the three cycles are problematic.

The historical-continuous method is an approach that teaches the three cycles are three separate scenes in history and follow one another linearly. The criticism of this view is that each cycle seems to be self-contained. The recapitulation method is an approach that postulates that each cycle is self-contained, but each of the three cycles is describing the same scene. The main criticism of this approach is that there are differences in the three cycles. For example, the seven seals affect one-fourth of the earth. The seven trumpets judged one-third of the earth, and with the seven bowls, all of the earth was judged. In each group of cycles, John is talking about judgment. The cycles may not be the same; however, God's wrath intensifies with each cycle. This is God's judgment against an apostate humanity.

The first two cycles (seals and trumpets) share common characteristics. The first four elements of the two cycles present a concise description of catastrophe. The fifth and sixth sections are more elaborate descriptions with intensification of the events. An interlude occurs in the seventh section, and the first element in the first new cycle begins. The third cycle of bowl judgment is separated by four chapters of material. A pattern of seven like the first two cycles is not found here. The inference here is that judgment does not always coincide with absolute boundaries.

The seven seals begin with the four horsemen of the apocalypse. On the first seal, the rider of the white horse (refers to the Parthians) carries a bow, wears a crown and appears as a conqueror, especially of the poor. On the second seal, there is a rider on a bright red horse who removes peace from the earth. Red is a color of conflict and war. With the third seal, the rider is riding on a black horse and holds a pair of scales.

John heard what sounded like a voice among the four living creatures saying, "Two pounds of wheat for a day's wages, and six pounds of barley for a day's wages, but do not damage the oil and the wine." This is inflation after war and seems to indicate that the poor always suffer more than the wealthy during hard times. On the fourth seal, death was riding on a pale green horse and Hades followed closely behind him. They were given power over a fourth of the earth to kill by sword, famine and plague, and by the wild beasts of the earth. The message here may be that evil is self-destructing.

With the fifth seal, John saw under the altar the souls of those who had been slain because of the Word of God. The martyrs are not in Heaven seeking revenge. They have already died and are enjoying their reward. They want God's will and justice to be done. Under the altar is a reference to sacrifices in the temple. Life, soul, spirit, and the self are all interchangeable in this context. Animal sacrifices are gifts to God. Martyrs are sacrificed for God.

The sixth seal is a sign that judgment by God is taking place. The earth quakes, the sun turns black, the moon turns red, the stars fall; people hide from the wrath of the Lamb.

With the seventh seal, silence fills Heaven for a half hour before an angel hurls a censer with fire to earth and seven angels blow trumpets. The reader of Revelation would have known that God was in control. This leads into the judgment of the seven trumpets.

In the first trumpet, hail, fire and blood hurl down on earth; one-third of earth is burned. In the second trumpet, a burning mountain bloodies and destroys one-third of the sea, its creatures and its ships. In the third trumpet, a star called Wormwood turns one-third of the fresh water bitter; many people die because of their unfaithfulness. In the fourth trumpet, one-third of the sun, moon and stars become dark.

With the fifth trumpet, a star falls to earth and opens the Abyss, releasing locusts like scorpions who torture the unsaved (the oppressors of the Christians) for five months. "They had as king over them the angel of the Abyss, whose name in Hebrew is Abaddon and in Greek is Apollyon, destroyer" (Rev 9:11). Apollyon is a pawn for the Greek God, Apollo. Domitian called himself Apollo. The locust was the symbol for Apollo.

In the sixth seal, an army led by four angels kills one-third of humankind. "The rest of mankind who were not killed by these plagues still did not repent of the work of their hands; they did not stop worshiping demons, and idols of gold, silver, bronze, stone and wood--idols that cannot see, hear, or walk. Nor did they repent of their murders, their magic arts, their sexual immorality or their thefts" (Rev. 9:20-21).

John was instructed to seal up what the voices of the seven thunders had said, and not write it down. In apocalyptic writing, God always shortens the time of persecution for his people. The seventh seal, the kingdom of the world becomes the kingdom of Heaven; God's temple opens and reveals the Ark of the Covenant. Next is a four-chapter interlude before the seven bowls of God's wrath.

Typical of apocalyptic literature is that the author describes the flow of history from one time of persecution to current persecution. The purpose is to show how present evil developed and evolved.

The bowl judgments remind the readers of Exodus in Egypt. In the first bowl, those with the mark of the beast who worships its image break out in sores. With the second bowl, the sea turns to blood that kills all life in it. In the third bowl, the waters turn to blood. The penalty of sin should be appropriate for that particular sin (Rev. 16:6). With the fourth bowl, the sun scorches people with fire, and in the fifth bowl, darkness covers the beast's kingdom; people gnaw their tongues and curse God.

In the sixth bowl, an angel poured out his bowl on the great river Euphrates, and its water was dried up to prepare the way for the kings from the East to assemble for battle. This assembling takes place at Armageddon. This city does not exist. Armageddon may be a reference to the city Megiddo. Ancient Jewish history records significant battles fought at or near Megiddo. Further, after the gathering of the kings for battle, God spoke and destroyed his enemies with his mouth. No battle was fought.

In the seventh bowl, an angel poured out his bowl into the air, and out of the temple came a loud voice from the throne, saying, "It is done!" An earthquake splits the great city; one-hundred-pound hailstones fall on people. The battle had already been fought and won in Chapter 5 of Revelation. The slaughtered lamb has already conquered death. This was the final battle that humans and the cosmos faced. Therefore, another battle was not indicated. Nevertheless, Armageddon symbolizes a place where the power of God defeats the forces of evil.

In the final analysis, John believed that he was describing the soon-to-come final return of Jesus. John was mistaken since this is not supported by the material in Revelation. The book was not written for the distant future, since it would not help the people who were addressed then. They would have no hope and no reason to remain faithful if it had nothing to do with them.

A contrasting view is to propose that John did not understand himself to be describing Jesus' final return. John was concerned with the end of persecution in his day (94-95 CE). Domitian died in 96 CE. After Domitian's death, persecution of Christians ceased in that part of the world. For John, the end of persecution was near, but had a little longer to go. If this view is accurate, then John was exactly right. His whole appeal then was to remain faithful in the midst of hard times.

Deliverance was around the corner. Satan would have to die. A special reward would be given to those who remain faithful. The consequence of unfaithfulness, the second death, is the same today as it was in 94-95 CE. Revelation is a book of hope; it promises a reward for the faithful (everlasting life) and a reward for the unfaithful (a second death).

Again, Revelation is a book of hope. "...in your hearts revere Christ as Lord. Always be prepared to give an answer to everyone who asks you to give the reason for the hope you have" (NIV 1 Peter 3:15). To have hope, it seems to me that one would need to know God and relate to him.

So, the question becomes, how do we know God is real outside of his son Jesus in the New Testament? If God is real, how does mankind relate to him? For these questions, this writer will employ a factitious dialogue between Thomas Aquinas and Martin Luther to deal with some theological arguments that should shed light on this concept.

Endnotes - Chapter IV: Revelation

1. James Efird, Revelation for Today: An Apocalyptic Approach (Nashville, Abingdon Press, 1989), 25.
2. James Efird, Revelation for Today: An Apocalyptic Approach (Nashville, Abingdon Press, 1989), 25.
3. Bart Ehrman, The New Testament: A Historical Introduction to The Early Christian Writings (New York, Oxford University Press, 2012), 458-459.
4. James Efird, Revelation for Today: An Apocalyptic Approach (Nashville, Abingdon Press, 1989), 56.

Clemmie Palmer, III, MD

Chapter V: Relating to God

Dialogue

Dr. Grace, president of the famous Middle Age School of Theology in central Europe, is recruiting a professor to teach theology at this University. The most important criteria for this prestigious position is adequately teaching the assurance of salvation. Ninety-five percent of the students at Middle Age indicated during a recent survey that they struggle with their own salvation.

On the surface, it appears that these students are content in all areas of their lives; they are all products of noble families. The remaining five percent are not of nobility nor do they have bionic enhancements. Further, this population (ninety-five percent of the students) have unusual physical talents; bionic eyes, bionic ears, exceptional sense of smell and taste, as well as extra sensory receptors which enhance knowledge acquired by touch. In short, these students want to be assured that their salvation lies completely in the hands of God.[1] The students have enough on their minds and should not have to worry about their salvation since the tuition is a $100,000 a semester per Dr. Grace.

The interview has certain rules that must be followed. It will be in the form of a boxing debate and no clapping or loud noise is allowed. There are many people at the debate. They give themselves several names: Scholastic Theologians, Protestants, Catholics and more. The total number in the audience is about 144,000. There is another number no man can count, sitting in a section called the second Heaven. The 144,000 represent the 12 departments of this university. Each department head has a vote and the student body votes only in case of a tie.

The debate takes the form of a three-round boxing match. If one participant is knocked out, then the debate is obviously terminated, and a winner is deemed. If the fight goes the distance, then the 12 judges and the president will go into the upper room, called the Opera trinitatis ad extra indivisa sunt room, where voting occurs.

Each round lasts ten minutes and both parties must answer questions from Dr. Grace and can respond to comments from the audience. Only once in the three-round bout can a participant ask their opponent a direct question. There is a two-minute break after each round giving the candidates time to confer with their team.

Dr. Grace:	Thomas Aquinas, you were selected to go first by the flip of the coin.
Audience:	Complete silence.
Dr. Grace:	[Round 1] Who influenced you the most, academically?
Aquinas:	I would say Aristotle because of his reasoning skills.
Luther:	I would say the Apostle Paul since he wrote that we are justified by faith. However, I believe that man is justified by faith alone, for clarity.

Audience:	Some are clapping, others booing. The clapping is mainly from the large student body.
Dr. Grace:	[Had to calm the audience and threaten to remove some from the room.]
Judges:	[Some were thinking, Luther added to the Bible.] Does he think he has the right to do that?
Others:	Well, Aquinas did not mention Paul; he mentioned Aristotle, a philosopher. A few judges asked themselves, "Does Paul need clarity?"
Aquinas:	[His team advised him to ask Luther a question.] Mr. Luther, did God authorize you to change Paul's teaching by adding alone to Paul's writing?
Luther:	The God I know talks or reveals himself to humans, but let me ask you a question… Your question indicated to me that you really do not know God. How do you know God exists?
All Judges:	[Say to themselves, "It is getting interesting now."]
Dr. Grace:	[Round 2] The topic for round two is about the existence of God.
Aquinas:	Whether I know God exists or not does not give you the right to change the Bible. Audience and distinguished faculty, we learn through our five senses. Think of a cause and effect on a topic like motion. [Aquinas throws his pen on the floor.]

	Something had to cause this pen to move. One can say that I caused it to move. Then one may ask, who causes me to move?
	If one follows this cause and effect logic back to infinity, then at some point an unmoved mover will be deduced. Thus, I am able to say with confidence that an unmoved mover always existed who cannot be acted upon or moved. Therefore, God, the unmoved mover, exists. Luther, we should be able to come together based on reasoning.
Luther:	Interrupting Aquinas, can you explain the Trinity based on reasoning?
Audience:	[Becomes loud again.]
Dr. Grace:	Guards, please escort these eighty-two students right here [pointing to his left] to room 1521. That room, known as The Worms, is equipped with audio-video technology so they can see the debate. After their next offense, they will lose their right to vote.
Judge Modalist:	Likes Luther's question and can hardly wait to hear Aquinas' response.
Aquinas:	For the record, Luther has broken a rule. He has already asked me one direct question, now he is asking another one on the Trinity.
Dr. Grace:	He is right Luther. One point will be deducted from your score.
Luther:	Yes, Sir.

Aquinas:	I will answer the question posed by Luther anyway.
Judge Basil:	Started sweating… said to himself, if he answers this one correctly then he will earn my vote.
Aquinas:	On one level man can talk about God since this level is based on the natural world and reasoning through our five senses. However, there is another level in which God has to reveal himself to man, which requires faith. Therefore, the answer to Luther's question is no.
Judge Modalist:	I like Aquinas answer, but I wish we had another candidate because both are talking about a Trinity. Three persons will certainly not relieve salvific anxiety for these students.
Judge Tri-Theist:	I agree.
Judge Isaiah and Judge Jeremiah:	(Look at each other in unbelief. Jeremiah becomes tearful.)
Judge Trinity:	(Judge Trinity, the newest member of the faculty, was sitting at the table with several other judges: Dr. Paul of Samosata, Dr. Martyr and Dr. Docetists. Martyr advised Judge Modalist to conceal his comments until the upper room to show unity among the faculty.)
Dr. Grace:	I know that it is Luther's turn, but I would like to start round three with Aquinas if it

	is approved by Judge Tertullian, the University's legal counsel.
Judge Tertullian:	(Thinking to himself. We do not need a philosopher in the position.) "That is acceptable Dr. Grace.
Dr. Grace:	[Round 3] Is salvation available on the level of the natural world?
Aquinas:	No. The fact that God loves man is concluded by grace through faith which is an act of revelation.
Dr. Grace:	I'm sorry, Luther. According to Judge Origen, who wrote the debate disciple, we are running short on time. Please make your response brief. What do you think about Aquinas' seemingly two-tier approach to the knowledge of God?
Judge Augustine:	Probably the most respected member of the faculty is thinking, I am glad God monergistically influenced Dr. Grace to ask that question.
Luther:	I have one objection, also. My opponent went over his ten-minute limit in round two.
Dr. Grace:	One point will be deducted from your score, Mr. Aquinas.
Aquinas:	Yes Sir.
Luther:	Briefly, Aquinas cannot talk about God on the basis of motion or the natural world unless he himself is God. Man only knows God through what God reveals to him. Man relates only to the God who came into

the world as a baby and died on the cross. Man cannot understand or relate to the unmoved God of the universe, who Aquinas invented. Fallen man does not have the capacity to reason well enough to make correct conclusions about God without the assistance of Revelation[3]. In short, if one cannot trust the messenger (natural world) then it is absurd to trust the message (knowledge of God). This invention is a lie. It is the devil's theology. Reasoning would never lead man to the cross (the theology of glory). Man would never have thought to invent God's death on the cross (the theology of the cross). That is how I know God is real.

The audience erupts in applause. Aquinas is knocked down but gets up before the count of seven. The fight ends, and the decision is in the hands of the judges.

The judges go to the upper room to deliberate. Everyone is awaiting the decision of the twelve judges. The faculty, the student body, the number no man could count are all noticing increased heart rates. One of the eighty-two students in the Worms room stated, "We would not be in this predicament if we had different hearts (bionic hearts) which could unconditionally accept our security in Christ."

Dr. Grace announces that the judges have made their decision. The vote is a tie; six judges vote for Aquinas and six vote for Luther. Most of the people in the audience are shocked since Luther scored a knock down in round three. The decision is now in the hands of the student body.

The 95 percent of the student body is completely split down the middle. Ironically, this means that five percent (those that are not of nobility nor had bionic senses) of the remaining student body will choose the next professor! This five percent group, led by James Works, states that Luther may not have actually represented Paul correctly by adding the word "alone" after the faith argument.

James and his friend, Pistis Christou, feel that good works because of faith could decrease redemptive anxiety. The five-percent of the student body likes hearing this and votes for Aquinas. However, before Aquinas is inaugurated as the next professor, a challenge comes from the 82 students who had been confined to room 1521. They claim their audio-video equipment malfunctioned, and, therefore, their votes had not been counted.

Therefore, Dr. Grace, after a heated discussion with Judge Tertullian, decides to call the match a draw at the Middle Age School of Theology. I write, and you decide.

The winner of this match is not the point here. The intricate details are presented so that readers can see and have an appreciation of the issues that are important when one asks themselves the question about the existence of God and how to relate to God.

God, the World, and Me

Of note is the fact that five percent of the student body almost hired a new professor. This does not mean that they were right; it does mean that politics, the art of persuasion and worldly influence helped shape theological viewpoints. Dr. Grace decided to deliver a speech to calm the students at the Middle Age School of Theology. The students chanted that they wanted to see another match or another crisp dialogue on salvation. Nevertheless, Dr. Grace began his speech.

Speech

What is your stand on the origin of sin? Sin is defined in the classical Christian tradition as the universal and the hereditary sinfulness of man since the fall of Adam. It is contrasted with actual sin, which is the self-conscious violation of God's law. The ancient church struggled with the doctrine of sin and evil. Many people today place the fault of sin on God, Adam and Eve, or mankind independent of Adam and Eve. Augustine believed that certain views of evil were incompatible with the Christian faith. The church condemned the Manichean heresy for its theological pessimism and the Pelagian heresy for its anthropological optimism concerning evil.[4]

The church did not fully endorse the Augustine view of original sin, but its impact was so great that it has had an enormous influence on Western theology. Augustine's work on sin and evil came out of the Pelagius and Gnostic controversy. The fact that the church did not adopt Augustine's work officially indicates the fervor that Pelagius had on the subject. Augustine did not invent the doctrine of sin, but he expressed it systematically by drawing from scripture, his experiences, and Plato.

Pelagius viewed sin as a choice. Against this view, Augustine said that sin is a corruption of human nature that is inherited from Adam. He believed that man was totally depraved and powerless to make moral choices. God must act first for salvation, but man cannot resist a heart that has been chosen by God. For Augustine, man will respond favorably to God because he is elected. Pelagius did not believe in inherited sin and he taught that grace was unnecessary to move the will of man to accept God. Against the Gnostic, Augustine wrote that sin is not identifiable with human finitude. In other words, there is no ontological necessity of sin or God is not the author of sin.

There is a direct correlation between sin and salvation such that neither can be understood without the other. As we study the bible or oracles of God, all men and women must deal with the question of salvation once sin has been defined. The concept of salvation must be settled in our minds in order for one to be assured in our spirit. In other words, without the assurance of salvation one is lead down the road of anxiety. *What if, how much, can I,* and so forth, types of questions dominate the psyche. There is no inner peace!

Now, one can be saved at this level of spirituality but will not be solid. This use of solid means being self-aware that you know God personally and are subsequently self-assured of your salvation. This reminds me of the song:

"Yes, God is Real. There are some things, I may not know. There are some places I can't go, but I am sure of this one thing that God is real for I can feel him deep within. Yes, God is real, Yes, real in my soul, Yes God is real for he has washed and made me whole; for his love for me is like pure gold. Yes, God is real for I can feel Him in my soul…"

(The student body and the whole faculty is intensely listening.)

(Dr. Grace continues)

Now let us look at what I call a Scriptural Modality, which leads to salvation and what John Wesley called The Scriptural Way of Salvation. Faith and salvation are the marrow, which is the main component of a dissected Scripture. What is faith? Faith is divine evidence or conviction, not perceived by our external senses or modalities. "It is a kind of spiritual light exhibited to the soul, and a supernatural sight or perception thereof."[5]

Faith in that God was in Christ, reconciling the world unto himself and that Christ loved me and gave himself for me. It is through faith that we receive Christ as our Savior and Lord. God's spirit is witness to our spirit that we are children of God (assurance). Faith is the only condition of justification. Faith is divine evidence that we are saved from sin.

Further, it is also divine conviction that God is able to perform what he promises to purify man and fill his heart with holiness, and that God is able to do it now. There should be so much love in your heart that it does not leave any room for sin.

Think of a glass filled to the brim with water. At this point, one cannot pour anything else into the glass. From time to time, some of this water may evaporate and a liquid called sin might enter. This liquid sin will not make up the majority of the glass' contents. More love will dilute and eventually replace it back to a heart filled with love.

Audience: Interruption… Several students wearing t-shirts with these names Beza, Barth, Arminius, and Newton on them, among others, shouted, "We somewhat understand sin now but want more on salvation."

One of the students asked, "What about Romans Chapter 9 or Ephesians Chapter 1?"

Endnotes - Chapter V: Relating to God

1. Paul Capetz, God: A Brief History (Minneapolis: Fortress Press, 2003), 90-96.
2. William Anderson, ed., A Journey Through Christian Theology (Minneapolis: Fortress Press, 2010), 172-173.
3. Roger Olson, The Story of Christian Theology: Twenty Centuries of Tradition & Reform (Downers Grove: IVP Academic, 1999), 384-387.
4. Peter Hodgson and Robert King, Christian Theology: An Introduction to Its Traditions and Tasks (Minneapolis, MN: Fortress Press, 1994), p 194.
5. Albert Outler and Richard Heitzenrater, John Wesley's Sermons: An Anthology (Nashville, TN: Abingdon Press, 1991), p 374.

Clemmie Palmer, III, MD

Chapter VI: Election

Dr. Grace abruptly ended his speech. He decided to invite three adjunct professors at the Middle School of Theology to discuss human salvation in Christ in a fictitious narrative about Rip Van Winkle which he hoped would give the students what they needed to at least curtail the shouting and, at best, calm salvific anxiety. All participants agreed to the meaning and usage of the following theological concepts before the next discussion was arranged.

Supralapsarianism

This 17th century reformed theological view expounds that God elected two groups (the elect and everybody else) before creation. God ordained the fall of man. The atoning death of Christ was for the elect (limited atonement), which represents God's mercy. The 'everybody else' group represents God's Justice, which is eternal punishment.

Infralapsarianism

Infralapsarianism is a 17th century reformed theological view that God created man first, then ordained the fall. Subsequently, God elected two groups (the elect and everybody else). The atoning death of Christ was for the elect (limited atonement), which represents God's mercy. The 'everybody else' group represents God's justice, which is eternal punishment.

Arminian Theology

God created man. Man fell. This fall was not ordained by God. The fall was the result of human decision. The atoning death of Christ is for all. Those who place their trust in Jesus have salvation in Christ. This represents God's love and mercy. Those who do not place their trust in Jesus get God's justice, which is eternal punishment.

Wesley's theology is based on Arminian theology. One can say that the elect group is based on the foreseen faith of believers. Salvation is only for believers who can lose it. This is contrasted with the sublapsarianism position. Those who believe are elected. Salvation applies only to believers who cannot lose it.

Discussion - Rip Van Winkle II

He had a nagging wife who was obsessed with Romans Chapter 9 and she suggested that he added the II to his name on his birth certificate because she believed that Romans Chapter 9 was about two groups and not individuals. She did not believe that her nagging was foreordained by God, which meant, to her, that she was predestined to Hell.

Rip Van Winkle II fell asleep for hundreds of years and was trying to capture parts of a dream to make a concise argument regarding salvation. Before Rip fell asleep, he was introduced to the teachings of Augustine, original sin, but was not settled on the issue of salvation. All of Rip's comments are silent and are for narrative effect.

Rip:	I remember that I was on a plane, the Enlightenment 747.
Pilots:	The copilot, Descartes, asked the pilot, Newton, "How should we fly this plane today?" Newton replied, "Since we have this great technology, let it go on autopilot."
Rip:	I also remember that Theodore Beza, Jacob Arminius, and Karl Barth were on the plane flying first class. Interesting, there was another man who I heard always rode coach and who was described as a person with extra-sensory perception; some described him as a liberationist, some say transcendent, and some say immanent. It is getting hard to remember the details. I heard the most interesting conversation among Beza, Arminius, and Barth. The other man who always rode coach heard everything and did not directly contribute anything verbally, but he seemed to communicate by prayer mostly. I do not really know. For practical purposes, I will call him JC."
Beza:	Members of the first-class section let us talk about God.
Rip:	Arminius, originally called a heretic by some, was reluctant to participate but liked the subject.
Barth:	Was busy writing his own systematic theology but desperately wanted to participate. He

decided to wait awhile to participate in the conversation about God giving respect to his elders and giving him time to cultivate a relationship with the mysterious JC.

Arminius: What in particular would you like to discuss about God?
Beza: Does God have a purpose in everything?
Arminius: Are you really asking about the order of divine decrees?
Beza: [Smiling] I think that God has a purpose in everything.
Arminius: Meaning everything good and bad?
Beza: Yes.
Arminius: You sound exactly like John Calvin.
Beza: I will take that as a compliment.
Arminius: [Laughing] Humans are so subjective.
Barth: [Sensing that the conversation was tilting toward predestination.] Beauty (thinking the truth) is in the eye of the beholder.
Arminius: Say what you really feel, Barth.
Barth: I just did, Sir.
Beza: [Smiling] As the head of the Genevan Academy and defender of the Reformed Protestant Position, I would like to assert that God is a logical and all-knowing God. Do you gentlemen agree?
Arminius: Certainly.
Barth: I agree.
Beza: So, if he is logical, then he created the world in a logical manner. Agree?

God, the World, and Me

Arminius: Silence.
Barth: Are you talking chronological here, Beza?
Beza: No, I am talking about logical order. The big picture.
Arminius: Hmmm, I see...
Beza: God foreordains everything that happens since he decrees it from eternity.
Arminius: Are you suggesting that God decreed the fall of Human beings?
Beza: Yes, and I am not budging on this position.
Arminius: Why can you not view this in a different way? I thought academic theologians always remain open to different points of view.
Barth: [He was really enjoying the dialogue but was more interested, at this moment, in completing his own systematic theology so kept quiet on Arminius' remark.]
Beza: God determines who is going to receive and not receive the gospel and it is totally out of human control.
Arminius: This comment and your comment on the fall sound like Supralapsarianism.
Beza: Exactly, mankind can only be saved, justified by Grace and not by works. If man had a choice to accept the gift of grace that saves, then man would be co-savior. It is about God not man.
Arminius: Beza... if God caused the fall, then God is the author of sin.

JC: [A loud sound came out of the coach section of the plane. Turbulence began at forty thousand feet in the air.]

Rip: I do not remember much of the turbulence, but I will attribute it to JC. The pilot, Descartes, told all the passengers to double check their seat belts.

Beza: Do you think that I am going to agree with you on this issue about God causing sin?

Arminius: This has to be the case if deductive reasoning is applied to your argument. Furthermore, Jesus died for all. Beza you are making Jesus a lie. Humans have a role to play in their own salvation.

Beza: You sound like a synergist. Maybe you are a Roman Catholic. Do not take us back to the days of contributing to your own salvation like Pelagius.

Rip: Pelagius is the only name he remembered other than Augustine before he went to sleep.

Arminius: Would you like to end the conversation Beza? There is no reason to be condescending.

Beza: I apologize. If you have an alternative view, present it now.

Arminius: God created humans with free will. The fall was a result of human decision. The atoning death of Jesus is for all. Everyone is solely dependent on God's grace for salvation. God presents all with prevenient grace which is universal and irresistible.

God, the World, and Me

Beza: The only thing that makes sense is the part about irresistible grace.

Arminius: Well, your view decrees some to Hell... let me finish.

Beza: At least in Hell it is for the glory of God.[1]

Rip: More turbulence on the plane, thought to be produced presumably by JC in the coach section.

Arminius: God does not want glory in Hell. He wants a synergistic relationship on earth.

JC: [The turbulence calmed.]

Barth: Thinking silently ... maybe this turbulence is God showing up in person judging this conversation.

Arminius: Do not pass out Beza. Only prevenient grace is irresistible. One can say no to justifying grace and sanctifying grace.

Beza: How is that possible Arminius?

Arminius: One can simply say, 'I am not putting my trust in Jesus.'

Barth: For the record, Beza, I feel that prevenient grace allows Arminius to avoid Pelagianism.

Arminius: Thank you, Barth.

Beza: I apologized earlier while you were writing...

Arminius: Let me summarize myself. Justifying and saving grace are resistible. The Holy Spirit taps into the human will by prevenient grace and the human will must cooperate by accepting the need of salvation and allowing God to give the gift of faith. God will not impose it, neither can

	humans earn it. Humans cannot do anything regarding salvation without the supernatural assistance of God's grace.[2]
Rip:	Hand claps were heard coming from the coach section.
Barth:	[Barth finishes writing his book just as the loud noise from the hand clapping started.]
Newton:	[A pilot and mathematician noted that the noise was so loud the plane started to shake.] Make sure all of the luggage on board is anchored because we are having another random event called turbulence.
Beza:	There are no random events.
Barth:	That is true. People are not randomly elected to Heaven or Hell either.
Beza:	What do you mean?
Arminius:	Wow.
Barth:	We all agree that God is logical, created man and knows everything. Therefore, God knew that man would fall. God elected Jesus Christ to be rejected so man could be elected and not rejected. Romans Chapter 9 is about two groups of people, the saved and the unsaved. Therefore, when you talk about predestination, you must run it through Jesus Christ. Jesus' death on the cross theoretically gives all men an opportunity to be saved.
Beza:	So, Barth, is everyone going to be saved? Are you a Universalist?
Barth:	The decision regarding who is saved is up to God. I have no jurisdiction over that.

Arminius: This is a good point. Barth. I would like to add one of my favorite verses to shed light on this issue which may crystalize your and my position, if I may.

Barth: Carry on Arminius.

Arminius: The Lord is not slow about his promise, as some think of slowness, but is patient with you, not wanting any to perish, but all to come to repentance (2 Peter 3:9).

Beza: [Talking under his breath] How do we get to repentance...

Barth: [Heard this barely audible question] I need some help with this one. [He decided to go to the coach area of the plane to ask JC about repentance. He finally made it to coach and met JC.]

Hi James. [Dr. James Cone, an African American systematic theologian, is the JC he so desperately wanted on his team.] How are you, James?

Cone: [Smiling] I am doing fine. Happy to be on this plane like everybody else.

Barth: Would you please join us in first class to talk about redemption?

Cone: Barth, can I bring Malcolm and Martin with me?

Barth: [Put his hand on Cones' shoulder] Awe, awe... Cone let's do that at another time.

Cone: I understand, and I will go briefly by myself then.

Barth: Thank you.

Cone: Gentlemen, you cannot have redemption until you understand the cross. I heard most of the conversation earlier. You all are focusing on reason. Liberal Protestantism is about reason and experience. You cannot achieve redemption until you link the crucifixion of Jesus to the lynching of Blacks. I read the Bible from the bottom up. God is God of the poor, helpless, and the marginalized. One then can ask for forgiveness of sins and achieve redemption.

Beza: I do not agree with that.

Cone: I know. People that do not agree with that are usually on the top. This is the way I see redemption through my story. I am interested in your story though. Everyone has to interpret the Gospel themselves and come to an understanding of the role Jesus is playing in their own lives now.

Barth: Well, the big picture... is that we all need some type of personal encounter with Jesus, at his discretion, to ask for forgiveness and therefore become redeemed.

[At this remark all the men agree and the plane landed safely.]

Rip: [Rip finally awakens after hundreds of years. He realized that he missed years of Christian debate. Man had gone from total depravity to the enlightenment. From the enlightenment to talking about a personal encounter with Jesus.

The students' question about salvation was answered. Man can go directly to God by way of the cross to ask for forgiveness in order to attain salvation. Rip's wife also realized that she did not have to view Romans Chapter 9 as if it was God. She learned that if she wants to know God, then all she has to do is go directly to the cross. After this flight, she asked her husband Rip to change his name back to his original name since she learned that everyone who calls on the name of the Lord shall be saved.] (Romans 10:13)

Dr. Grace: I would like to thank all participants of this discussion and make a few comments on God's thinking and his decrees. According to Dr. Norman Geisler, God's thoughts are not arranged in a linear sequence, as one is dependent on the other. "All thoughts are known by God in one eternal co-intuition. As a simple Being, He therefore knows all things simply, which is why the Bible speaks of election as being 'in accordance with' His will (Eph. 1:5, 1 Peter 1:2) and not based on or independent of other attributes.[3]

For another view of redemption outside of Barth and Cone, let us consider Schleiermacher in the next chapter. This writer does not necessarily agree with his view, but this represents another example of how politics, the art of persuasion, and the world influence theological thought.

Endnotes - Chapter VI: Election

1. Roger Olson, The Story of Christian Theology: Twenty Centuries of Tradition & Reform (Downers Grove: IVP Academic, 1999), 459.
2. Roger Olson, The Story of Christian Theology: Twenty Centuries of Tradition & Reform (Downers Grove: IVP Academic, 1999), 471.
3. Norman Geisler, Systematic Theology in One Volume (Minneapolis, MN: Bethany House, 2011), 816-817.

Chapter VII: Another View of Redemption

Friedrich Schleiermacher (1768-1834), who is widely regarded as the father of modern theology, believed that one learns by way of an inner-outer dialectic. In order for learning to take place a transaction has to occur. This is the framework in which God, in his sovereignty, expresses himself through Jesus Christ and the church. When humanity connects to Jesus, it has by a willful, gracious, and unforced transaction through love bonded with God.

In other words, this dialectic enabled Schleiermacher to present a theological work, which explains how God is revealed and how he accomplishes redemption through Jesus. Moreover, this redemption is being carried out today through the Holy Spirit. For Schleiermacher, "the Holy Spirit, conceived as the common spirit of the church, is the same thing as 'Christ in us,' the same thing as Christ's continuing presence in and through the church after Jesus' death."[1] Schleiermacher viewed Jesus' life, not his death or resurrection, as redemption itself.

In order for an experience to have meaning, a transaction, which facilitates meaning, must take place. In essence, a dialogue between at least two beings must occur. This dialogue can be explicit as well as implicit. According to Schleiermacher, oscillations (the back and forth processing of information) occur whenever external material is brought into the self. This is analogous to the Psychoanalytic development theory today with terms like introjection, projection, internalization and identification. Through this process, one becomes conscious of an external reality. Humanity is said to have God-consciousness when humanity experiences God through Jesus, who has perfect God-consciousness through the process of oscillations. Jesus, unlike humanity, did not have to wrestle with truth from an external source. God incarnated God's spirit in Jesus.

This is critically important to the Christian faith. On the other hand, stepping outside of this dialogue leads one to understand that there is an awareness, according to Schleiermacher of an independent influence upon mankind. We are absolutely dependent on this one.[2]

In Christianity, we learn to call this one "God." Schleiermacher believed that every human being has a conscious awareness of the influence of God. "Christ is just like us except that he was able to do perfectly what we did not know we could do... until we experienced redemption."[3]

Schleiermacher, in *Christian Faith*, defined redemption as "in this collective life which goes back to the effectiveness of Jesus, redemption is effected by Him through the communication of His sinless perfection."[4]

Redemption is brought about by Jesus sharing his sinless perfection. This definition does not include Jesus' death or resurrection. Mankind can be brought into this sinless perfection by a salvific relationship with Jesus as a gift of grace from God. When mankind recognizes the sinless perfection of Jesus, at least three things happen: (1) mankind's sin is made clearer, (2) mankind realizes that

God, the World, and Me

Jesus can free mankind from sin, and (3) the Redeemer takes up the faithful into the power of his God-consciousness, and this is his redeeming activity. Everything that is achieved through the process of redemption is accomplished by Jesus' sinless perfection. [5] Let us take a closer look at sin through the lens of Schleiermacher.

Most Christians were taught the "rules" of life from the church, from the Commandments, or from cultural norms. Many Christians think of redemption as being redeemed from sin. Sin is traditionally defined as the transgression of God's law or all wrongdoing, etc. Schleiermacher's view of sin is anything that impedes the development of God-consciousness. Man is not aware of sin until man is aware of redemption. The experience of redemption defines sin. In contrast to the classic view of redemption by many Christians, Schleiermacher looked at redemption as what we are redeemed for which is communion with God.

One does not know God-consciousness is possible until one knows what prevents it from developing, which is grace. Therefore, the awareness of sin comes after the awareness of grace.[6] Grace gives man the possibility of an intimate relationship with God.

Moreover, "man's relationship with God is never perfect. Sin is always present. Grace and sin are always modifying each other in Christians as our openness to intimate relationship with God grows and diminishes through the events of our lives."[7] This is the difference between Jesus and mankind. Jesus had complete receptivity of God-consciousness all the time. God-consciousness will be examined through a discussion of God, Jesus, and the church.

According to Schleiermacher, God is complete, sovereign, and non-personal. God cannot be directly lured into the temporal world, though he chooses to work in and through it. God created Jesus. "There is no historical pre-existence of either the divine or the human in the nature of Jesus before it happened historically in the land of Palestine. … One can say that Jesus always existed in the mind of God."[8]

Since the existence of Jesus, prior to his birth, has been excluded, one can surmise that God freely decided to intervene in the world by incarnating his God-consciousness into Jesus for the purpose of redemption from bondage. When a person is not conscious of an absolute dependence on God, they are in a state of bondage. Bondage, sinful state, and alienation from God are all covariant concepts.

Schleiermacher rejected the orthodox view that Jesus is the second person of the trinity. Jesus is the Son of God, not God the Absolute. God gave Jesus perfect God-consciousness. This is another way of saying the Absolute was in Jesus or God became human in Jesus. This does not mean that Jesus' thoughts were robotic in nature. Jesus had his own thoughts as a human being.

Jesus' thoughts and actions were positively correlated with the God-consciousness in him. Jesus' perfect, sinless

God-consciousness is God's work in history. Jesus did not become God and did not have two natures. For Schleiermacher, divinity means God's active presence in human consciousness.[9] God is present in Jesus, human consciousness, and the church.

Scripture is not the foundation of Christian faith. Faith in Christ must occur before Scripture can attain special authority.[10] The experience of redemption is the same for mankind now as it was for Jesus' first followers. Further, the first followers of Jesus did not have Scripture as the backbone of their faith. Faith passed from person to person in the church by the living witness of redemption expressed by behaviors that exemplify God-consciousness. "Scripture alone, without the church's witness to the living experience of redemption, would be lifeless."[11]

Schleiermacher did not consider the resurrection as part of the redeeming activity of Jesus. The resurrection was not an act of Jesus, but of God. Schleiermacher wrote that God-consciousness, which was perfected in Jesus, was not proved or influenced by the resurrection. Thus, the resurrection is inconsequential as it relates to redemption.[12] Moreover, the resurrection is not a logical outcome after the death of the one who redeems by perfect God-consciousness.

Last, the first followers of Jesus recognized him as the Son of God. This meant that they had experienced redemption before Jesus' death and resurrection. If Christ's death and resurrection was part of his redeeming activity, the true recognition of Jesus as the Son of God would not have been possible.

This in no way means that Schleiermacher did not endorse the resurrection. He displayed the same type of thinking about the resurrection as he did in the teaching of redemption. If a person believes in the Gospel account of the resurrection, then one believes in the historical record of Jesus as written in the Gospel. However, this means that belief in a historical account of Jesus is not a test of faith. Schleiermacher alleged that a historical reason existed to support the resurrection. The same witnesses who spread the redemptive message during the first century and therefore assisted the next generation with redemption testified that Jesus was resurrected. Further, this same personal testimony and the Holy Spirit is the way in which Christ redeems today.

After Christ was resurrected and physically left to commune with his father, his work of redemption continued through the community of faith, the church. The logic is that Christ was an effective redeemer because of God in him. Christ's effectiveness in the church is, therefore, also because God is in it as the common Spirit of the church. Schleiermacher wrote, "The Holy Spirit could, as this common Spirit, only be fully communicated and received after the departure of Christ from the earth."[13]

Therefore, the Spirit of Christ and the Holy Spirit are synonymous, two ways of referring to a relationship with the church. Thus, being taken up into the life of Christ (redemption) and receiving the Holy Spirit on an individual level is the same thing. Schleiermacher thought that the doctrine of the Trinity (Father, Son, and Holy Spirit) was too speculative. He felt that this doctrine goes beyond human experience and human comprehension, if it was indeed true.

Schleiermacher taught the following: the Holy Spirit is the name we give to the being of God present in the community of faith, Jesus is the name we give to the man who had perfect God-consciousness and ... that there is one being, God, who is the cause of redemption.[14]

Schleiermacher claimed that after the ascension of Jesus, the church, and the church only, became the vehicle in which redemption occurs. This is because the Holy Spirit works through Christians in the community of faith to evoke others to the experience of God-consciousness, which is redemption. Schleiermacher believed that the unregenerate starts his journey toward salvation in the church with the communication of Jesus' sinless perfection.

Blessedness is felt simultaneously with redemption. Therefore, blessedness is a byproduct of redemption as is experienced in a community of faith. Blessedness is the reward of true intimacy with God. As one assimilates more and more to Jesus' sinless perfection, one's blessedness becomes theoretically complete. This process is not merely individualistic, but is a corporate existence in the church.

God-consciousness of the contemporary Christian is based on the historical Jesus within a community of faith. "This new life (of redemption and blessedness) is not generated by the believer, or by the church itself, but is actually imparted through communion with Jesus in whom it has its source and who is its 'ideal' realization."[15]

The church, which is a fellowship of believers, is the medium by which Christ-perfect God-consciousness is taught and the sacraments are the means whereby the fellowship of believers with each other and with Christ is nourished.[16]

The world is outside the fellowship of Christ and, as such, cannot redeem. On the other hand, Schleiermacher kept the door of redemption open for all. The experience of redemption is one of the main reasons man knows the love of God. Those who have not yet been redeemed do not fully comprehend God's love. Their consciousness has not yet conceived God as loving them. "Even people who have some consciousness of God or some glimpses of grace cannot be said to recognize God's love for them, because the proper development of such a recognition can only come through the ministration of Christ and the Holy Spirit."[17]

This Trinitarian form used by Schleiermacher is not about a status of God in himself but is about the divine economy of redemption. It is simply a postulate which helps to explain God dealing with mankind. The Holy Spirit is the common community of the Church and as such a continuation of the presence of God in Jesus.[18]

Religious wars in the 17th century and the diversity of religious doctrines made many people challenge their religious views. Christian doctrine had become much less certain than the appealing logic of science. Modern science seemed to have excluded a view of divine intervention.

An intellectual movement given the title "the Enlightenment" was critical of orthodox Christianity on the grounds that it was irrational. Enlightenment thinkers used the terms *natural* and *revealed religion,* as they tried to understand the diversity of religions. Revealed religion is any religion based on revelation from God and nature religion is a religion based on reason. Natural religion disregarded the supernatural, miracles, divine intervention and incomprehensible dogma.

Schleiermacher cleverly appealed to the Enlightenment thinkers as well as to the Romantics by teaching that all human beings have an experiential awareness of the infinite God. This allowed the Enlightenment thinkers to reflect on spiritual issues without blind faith in church doctrine and possibly a sacrifice of the intellect.

It is this writer's view that Schleiermacher was influenced by Immanuel Kant. If Kant had challenged Schleiermacher's theology based on the evidence of God's existence, Schleiermacher could claim a universal sense of the divine that is within humanity. Moreover, Kant believed that the structure of consciousness gives structure to the world. Further, Kant, in his response to David Hume, stated there was in addition to phenomenological knowledge another form of knowledge, which he called noumenal, which is not subject to empirical validation but just as vital (soul, faith, freedom).

Schleiermacher viewed Jesus as a human being rather that God in the flesh. He certainly had more of an adoptionistic view of Jesus than an incarnational one. The end result of redemption is the same. The view of Jesus appears to argue that Jesus is the perfect Christian. However, Christians by Schleiermacher's definition are dependent on Jesus for God's consciousness. Therefore, Jesus is more than a perfect Christian. The concept of perfect God-consciousness explains a type of incarnation, but not without speculation itself. This was the same critique that Schleiermacher levied against orthodox doctrine like the Trinity, which he deemed too speculative.

The definition of the Holy Spirit is unsupernatural instead of the orthodox supernatural belief. Schleiermacher purported that since religion is a feeling, that it could be communicated by personal example. It is better caught than taught sounds good except for where to catch it (religion).

This writer disagrees with Schleiermacher's view that the church is the only place to internalize religion. This seems to limit the power and sovereignty of God to present the gift of grace to man anywhere. One must distinguish between what the Bible teaches and what the Bible records (slavery, polygamy etc.). The Bible records Jesus instituting the church, but it is not clear that the Bible teaches one has to be in the physical church to be redeemed.

One of the criminals on the cross with Jesus rebuked the other one after the first one told Jesus to save himself and them. "'... This man has done nothing wrong... Jesus, remember me when you come into your kingdom.' Jesus replied, 'Truly, I tell you, today you will be with me in Paradise'" (Luke 23:39-43). There is no mention of the church.

On the other hand, this could mean that a religious experience with Jesus is of a higher authority than the church and therefore the Bible. In fact, Schleiermacher claimed that the Bible was not an absolute authority. It was neither supernaturally inspired nor infallible. This brings him into direct conflict with 2 Timothy, "all scripture is inspired by God and is useful for teaching, for reproof, for correction, and for training in righteousness" (2 Timothy 3:16).

One can see why Schleiermacher had to have an obsession with God-consciousness since he did not believe in the inspired authority of the Bible or the Trinity as one God. In other words, he did not have anything else to stand on but a view of Jesus redeeming through God-consciousness since he excluded Jesus' death and resurrection from his redemptive theology.

This is contrasted to the Apostle Paul when he explained the resurrection to the Corinthians in the great city of Corinth: "and if Christ had not been raised (from the dead physically), your faith is worthless; you are still in your sins" (1 Corinthians 15:17). Schleiermacher presented an aspect of redemption through the consciousness of the Infinite but his theology appears unorthodox at best and speculative at worse when compared to the Apostle Paul's account of redemption.

It is academically encouraged to think critically on the major topics in the Bible. However, one must be careful not to change the Bible as one writes a theology since it would not be the Holy Bible. Moreover, one must also not read from an egocentric perspective and use the Bible to justify or partly justify their one-sided worldview. An example of this type of wrong happened historically in the Salem witch trials of 1692.

Endnotes - Chapter VII: Another View of Redemption

1. Terrence Tice, Schleiermacher (Nashville: Abingdon Press, 2006), 42.2. Friedrich Schleiermacher, The Christian Faith in Outline (Middletown: Forgotten Books, 2012), 7.
2. Catherine Kelsey, Thinking About Christ with Schleiermacher (Louisville: Westminster John Knox Press, 2003), 73.
3. Friedrich Schleiermacher, The Christian Faith in Outline (Middletown: Forgotten Books, 2012), 37.
4. Friedrich Schleiermacher, The Christian Faith in Outline (Middletown: Forgotten Books, 2012), 9.
5. Catherine Kelsey, Thinking About Christ with Schleiermacher (Louisville: Westminster John Knox Press, 2003), 59.
6. Catherine Kelsey, Thinking About Christ with Schleiermacher (Louisville: Westminster John Knox Press, 2003), 59.
7. Abraham Kunnuthara, Schleiermacher On Christian Consciousness of God's Work in History (Eugene: Pickwick Publications, 2008), 54.
8. Abraham Kunnuthara, Schleiermacher On Christian Consciousness of God's Work In History (Eugene: Pickwick Publications, 2008), 45-46.
9. Friedrich Schleiermacher, The Christian Faith in Outline (Middletown: Forgotten Books, 2012), 49.
10. Catherine Kelsey, Thinking About Christ with Schleiermacher (Louisville: Westminster John Knox Press, 2003), 89.

11. Catherine Kelsey, Thinking About Christ with Schleiermacher (Louisville: Westminster John Knox Press, 2003), 90.
12. Friedrich Schleiermacher, The Christian Faith in Outline (Middletown: Forgotten Books, 2012), 47.
13. Catherine Kelsey, Thinking About Christ with Schleiermacher (Louisville: Westminster John Knox Press, 2003), 99.
14. Keith Clements, Friedrich Schleiermacher: Pioneer of Modern Theology (San Francisco: Collins Liturgical Publications, 1987), 55.
15. Stephen Sykes, "The Sacraments," in Christian Theology: An Introduction to Its Traditions and Tasks, ed. Peter Hodgson and Robert King (Minneapolis: Fortress Press, 1994), 294.
16. Abraham Kunnuthara, Schleiermacher On Christian Consciousness of God's Work In History (Eugene: Pickwick Publications, 2008), 102.
17. Abraham Kunnuthara, Schleiermacher On Christian Consciousness of God's Work In History (Eugene: Pickwick Publications, 2008), 122.

Chapter VIII: Theological Nearsightedness

The Bible and therefore the government in New England declared witchcraft a crime. According to the King James Version of the Bible, it is written, "You shall not suffer a witch to live" (Exo. 22:18). Many theologians believe that this verse applies to Israel only and is not written for modern believers.

In fairness to History, in 1692 about two hundred women and men were charged with the crime of witchcraft. Nineteen were hanged, four died in prison awaiting trial, and one man refused to offer a plea and was killed by the weight of stone used in a failed attempt to extract a guilty plea from him.[1] It is this writer's view that the holistic view of church and state along with church conflict combined with a negative view of the marginalized as well as an egocentric view of theology caused the 1692 witchcraft hysteria in Salem.

Several events of the psychosocial, military, political, and religious sphere created tension for the Puritans and contributed to the 1692 witch panic. About two decades before 1692 there were two Native American raids. The first occurred in 1675 and the second began in 1689. The Puritans regarded Native Americans for the most part as the devil. The psychological impact of the war with the Native Americans may have put extreme emotional stress on the magistrates in New England. In other words, the magistrates may have been thinking that, "we had a difficult time defeating the Indians during these wars, but we will get the

Indians (translated to mean witches and therefore the devil) in the courtroom.

Another factor which led to anxiety and contributed to the witch hunt hysteria was the theology of the Puritans itself. The Puritans believed that their fate was determined before they were born. They looked for clues that they were part of the elect. They believed that they were elected to Heaven or Hell. The colonist expected God to provide for them in exchange for following His ordinances. In short, the Puritans believed that God dealt with them through covenants.

Dr. Vincent Stine, adjunct professor of political science at George Washington University, wrote that, "The state, invested with God's authority, used the legal code to define and update the covenant. ... The state also used its powers to intervene in religious disputes that could undermine internal unity." Specifically, ministers participated in the state trials and in turn the state asked ministers to weigh in on spectral evidence, which they initially affirmed as legal evidence. Maintaining social order was essential to the Puritan foundation. Now that the background has been laid, the hysteria itself will be examined.

Usually a person on the margins of society was accused of witchcraft and a trial ensued. Many were convicted on the basis of their perceived character, hearsay, what seemed to be probable cause. Allowing the witness to use spectral (apparitions) evidence seems to have been the most disturbing and unscientific for the educated and rational thinking man who was not as much impressed with supernatural arguments.

Church membership was another major issue for the Puritans. By the 1650s, church members were concerned about the growth of the church. Membership in the church was limited to those who could demonstrate that they had a personal relationship with God. Those who were able to demonstrate a personal relationship with God were considered part of the elect and therefore predestined to Heaven. Fewer people sought membership in church and over a period of time the church rolls declined.

The church had to answer the question, "What should be done with the children of baptized nonmembers?" The general court called for a synod of the clergy and lay church members in 1662. The consensus was the Half-Way Covenant. "This agreement allowed children to be baptized and brought into the church as long as their parents recognized the 'historic faith' of the church and demonstrated 'outward conformity' with God's teaching."

Reverend Parris viewed the 1662 ruling of Half-Way Covenant as liberal and only a non-spiritual means to increase membership. Parris did not agree with parents who did not want to testify in public about God's intervention in their lives. Reverend Parris saw this church polity issue as the devil's work. Many Salem village residents refused to join Reverend Parris' congregation. Reverend Parris preached sermons months before the witchcraft accusations began. His sermons were apocalyptic in nature, dividing the village into categories: the elect and the non-elect, the converted and the wicked, and his supporters and opponents.

"In his sacrament day sermon before the girls in his house voiced their initial accusations, Parris warned of Satan's attempt to 'pull down' his church—a charge tantamount to an accusation of witchcraft." Parris' opponents managed to prevent other villagers from joining the church. A village meeting, held on October 1691, made up of Parris' opponents voted to cut off Parris' pay and question his claim to the village parsonage and land.

It is not surprising given Parris' position in this conflict that the first to be affected by "agents of the devil" was in his household. This was viewed by many of the villagers, preachers, and magistrates as Satan's attack on a minister's family and that this attack would eventually metastasize to all the churches in New England. Governor Phips created special courts called, Oyer and Terminer, to hear the inordinate number of cases that resulted from church conflict labeled as "attacks of the devil" and masquerading as witchcraft accusations.

The witch hunt of 1692 started in the home of Reverend Samuel Parris in Salem, Massachusetts. It is important to note that young girls in Puritan society were to be seen and not heard and this may have contributed to the accusations of Salem Village girls. Although girls were to be seen and not heard, the accusers of Salem Village all belonged to families of prominent church members who feared the church was under attack by the devil. It was reported that

Tituba, a slave, who lived in the house of Reverend Parris told them witchcraft stories and performed magical rituals.

Reverend Parris' nine-year-old daughter, Elizabeth, and his eleven-year-old niece, Abigail William, began to have what appeared to be strange fits (crawled under chairs, made bizarre gestures, and made ridiculous speeches, etc.) Reverend Parris had the girls examined by Dr. Williams Griggs, a local physician. Dr. Griggs found no medical basis for their fits. He concluded that the girls must be under an evil spirit. Parris agreed with Dr. Griggs' assessment.

Even before Dr. Griggs had examined the girls, Reverend Parris, in a sermon, introduced the girls' affliction to the church. He stated that assistants of Satan were at work in Salem Village. This would certainly have constituted a formal charge of witchcraft if an individual was named.

It is this writer's opinion that the girls were influenced by Reverend Parris' sermons. After Dr. Griggs' examination, Mary Sibley, a neighbor of Parris and church member, told Parris' slave, John Indian, to make a witch cake from the children's urine and rye meal. This cake (a traditional English technique for identifying witches) would be fed to the dogs and burned with the result being that the girls would be able to name the witches.

According to Reverend John Hale's account, Tituba, one of Parris' slaves, admitted to making this cake. This certainly linked Tituba to witchcraft even though this gesture was generated by Mary Sibley. Puritans were diabolically against magic as the devil's work. However, they would consent to counter magic or what resource seemed helpful to them at a given moment in time in order to produce evidence for their own preconceived conclusions.

Reverend Parris stated that soon after John Indian and Tituba completed the witch cake procedure, the girls immediately started seeing apparitions and naming those who bewitched them. Therefore, it can be concluded that the girls must have known something about the witch cake procedure. Not only was the cake procedure in play, but Parris himself, under pressure from frightened neighbors regarding witchcraft, encouraged the girls to name their tormentors. The girls named Tituba, Sarah Good, and Sarah Osborne as their tormentors.

Moreover, the girls were initially reluctant to name the alleged witches. Some would argue that they may have been worried about vengeance. However, if it is assumed that the girls were telling lies, why would the accusations be difficult for them? It is logical to deduce that the girls in this male dominated society wanted to feel important and to please the respected males in this society by telling these men what they wanted to hear. The hesitancy to name the accusers gave the girls time to rehearse their story and time to know what kind of detail the men wanted in the stories.[5]

Tituba, a slave, was the perfect person for the girls to blame as a tormentor. She and her husband John were purchased by Reverend Parris in Barbados, during his residence there in the 1670s. Tituba had a reputation of practicing supernatural knowledge from her own country. She was described as an Indian. Along with the belief by Puritans that Native Americans worshiped the devil in addition to the history of Native American attacks, it is easy to see why Tituba was named. In 1692, Tituba confessed to the crime of witchcraft, which certainly intensified the witch hysteria and made matters worse for all the people who were accused.

Tituba knew her socioeconomic situation and that she was a scapegoat. She knew that denials would not impress the court. Tituba's only goal was to save her life through a false confession. Tituba reported that Good and Osborne were witches and described their specters in terms that the girls had already used. After a dramatic story to make her version believable, Tituba only admitted to pinching the girls, but only because she feared for her own life.

Further, the magistrates also introduced the Puritan concept of the devil's book (making a covenant with the devil) which Tituba reported as a fact. Eventually, Tituba recanted her confession in the fall of 1692. She remained in prison until April of 1693 until an unknown person paid her jail fines. Tituba and John's fate are a mystery.

The fate of Good and Osborne was also affected by the third girl to be afflicted, twelve-year-old Ann Putnam, Jr., daughter of Thomas and Ann Putnam, members of Reverend Parris' church. Ann was also the niece of Mary Sibley the instigator of the witch cake procedure mentioned earlier. "Like the other afflicted girls, Ann responded in court when prompted by the magistrates and performed her torments during the examination of Good, Osborne, and Tituba.

During Tituba's interrogation, she cried out that the previous night the specters of Good and Osborne tried to make 'hir cutt of hir own head.'"[6] Ann Putnam made a public confession on August 25, 1706. Diane Foulds, a descendant of one the people hanged in Salem and author, wrote that Ann's father initiated many of the formal complaints filed against suspected witches.[7]

Sarah Osborne, Sarah Good, and Tituba were jailed in Boston based on the orders magistrates Jonathan Corwin and John Hawthorne. Sarah Osborne and Sarah Good maintained their innocence until their death. Sarah Osborne was ill at the time of her arrest, never had a trial, and died of natural causes in prison on May 10, 1692. Sarah Good's trial was on June 28, 1692 and she was hanged on July 19, 1692.[8]

After twenty souls were executed, accusations were levied against men and women of spotless character. The witchcraft proceeding quickly came to an end when allegations were made against non-marginal and powerful citizens. The girls started to make accusations against men, children, and the upper class.[9] Rumors started that Increase Mather (Boston minister) and Governor Phips' wife were accused of witchcraft. Increase Mather outlawed spectral evidence, which led to the terminations of the proceedings. Governor Phips dissolved the court of Oyer and Terminer on October 29, 1692.

In conclusion, the events of 1692 in Salem are the result of what happens when a non-marginalized group projects neurotic fear to a marginalized group especially under the umbrella of religion. Dogmatic views of scripture are dangerous. Exodus 22:8 is the example of dogmatism which led in part to the 1692 witch trials.

The problem is that the Puritans did not want anyone to critique their view of theology. They created laws to keep egocentric harmony in their society. There was a lot of church and interpersonal conflict in Salem and these girls were used as pawns by Reverend Parris, Mr. Putnam, and the magistrates to further their own opinions about witchcraft without regard to the facts. Church conflict, interpersonal dis-ease, injustice toward the marginalized, neurotic fear, a belief in witchcraft, and a closed-minded religious body leads to death.

We should be open-minded and respectful of other's views. Isn't this a great way to heed the commission as Jesus told his 11 disciples in Matthew Chapter 26 to make disciples of all nations and to teach these disciples to obey everything that he taught them?

Next, I turn to C. S. Lewis' work for more on this subject.

Endnotes - Chapter VIII: Theological Nearsightedness

1. Richard Godbeer, The Salem Witch Hunt: A Brief History with Documents (Boston, Massachusetts: Bedford/St. Martin's, 2011), 1.
2. Vincent Stine, "A Church-State Partnership in Defense of the Puritan National Covenant," Journal of Church and State 56, no. 3 (February 2013): 501.
3. Vincent Stine, "A Church-State Partnership in Defense of the Puritan National Covenant," Journal of Church and State 56, no. 3 (February 2013): 494.
4. Benjamin Ray, "'The Salem Witch Mania': Recent Scholarship and American History Textbooks," Journal of the American Academy of Religion 78, no. 1 (March 2010): 47.
5. Peter Charles Hoffer, The Salem Witchcraft Trials: A Legal History (Lawrence, Kansas: University Press of Kansas, 1997), 55-56.
6. Benjamin Ray, Satan and Salem: The Witch-Hunt Crisis of 1692 (Charlottesville, Virginia: University of Virginia Press, 2015), 49.
7. Diane Foulds, Death in Salem: The Private Lives Behind the 1692 Witch Hunt (Guilford, Connecticut: Globe Pequot Press, 2013), 21.
8. Richard Godbeer, The Salem Witch Hunt: A Brief History with Documents (Boston, Massachusetts: Bedford/St. Martin's, 2011), 67-68.
9. Mark A. Noll, A History of Christianity in the United States and Canada (Grand Rapids, Michigan: Eerdmans, 1992), 51.

Chapter IX: Evangelism

C.S. Lewis' greatest goal was not fame and fortune, but to evangelize for the Christian faith. One does not have to be officially endorsed by a church body to be an effective evangelist. However, one has to have a clear, concise, and explainable argument regarding the Christian faith, once taught, maximized the conversion of the hearer. Next, this writer will document several techniques that C.S. Lewis used as an evangelist.

The first strategy to be considered is humility. One should never overestimate its importance. No one has a monopoly on God. People walk with the light that they have. I would implement this practice in my ministry setting because everyone deserves a place to stand. This does not mean that one should change one's position every time a controversial issue arises, but it does mean mutual respect should be the utmost strategy to spread the gospel. Just as important as humility, is the language that one uses.

The vernacular is the language of the people that one uses to teach and defend the Christian faith. Frequently, people in a teaching capacity—like theologians, physicians and attorneys—use the jargon of their field. Many times the communication is impaired. The intentions of the speaker do not meet the expectations of the listener. Talking in the vernacular of the listener eliminates the communication barrier. If one really wants to be a shepherd, one has to smell like sheep. Being around sheep teaches one to understand sheep. This leads to the next missiological strategy.

Evangelists need to know the other side of an argument. C.S. Lewis wrote in *Surprised by Joy* that he had been an atheist in a whirl of contradictions before he became a Christian. He knew the atheistic argument. He was asked his view on the materialists' and astronomers' argument regarding the accidental development of the planetary system and life. Lewis replied, "If the solar system was brought about by an accidental collision, then the appearance of organic life on this planet was also an accident, and the whole evidence of Man was an accident too... then the thoughts of materialism and astronomy are merely accidental by-products, why should I believe them to be true?" This will certainly be a major part of my missionary strategy so that my argument will not be diluted.

In addition, Lewis presents the Christian story or argument in an imaginative manner. Imagination is a nonthreatening technique to pre-baptize a child's imagination. *The Lion, the Witch, and the Wardrobe,* the first of *The Chronicles of Narnia* is a fairy tale that parallels Jesus atoning death for the sins of mankind. Briefly, four children (Peter, Susan, Lucy, and Edmund) entered into Narnia, a magic land with talking animals, animated trees, an evil white witch and a lion named Aslan.

Narnia was under the spell of the white witch resulting in the season being always winter and never Christmas. The white witch planned to execute Edmund because he violated the Deep Magic law instituted by the Great Emperor. Aslan was voluntarily killed in the place of Edmund. Moreover,

Aslan was resurrected. Here, Christianity was smuggled into fiction. Lewis also was interested in the pre-baptism of the adult's imagination.

The Great Divorce is an example of the pre-baptism of the adult's imagination. Lewis, in the common man's vernacular, wrote about what the church fathers called capital sins. The capital sins are gluttony, lust, greed, envy, sloth, anger, vanity and pride. Pride is the root of the capital sins.

There was a figurative bus tour made by the souls on earth to tour the outside of Heaven. All of the lost souls chose Hell because they did not effectively deal with their pride. Everyone must ultimately make a choice in life whether to seek Heaven or to enter Hell by free will. More on *The Great Divorce* later.

Lewis displayed in his writing style a unique ability to get the reader's attention by using what I call dualism. He makes the reader feel that a choice has to be made. Lewis implied in *The Weight of Glory* that intellectual and aesthetic activity is the flip side of a worse cultural life. "If you attempted... to suspend your whole intellectual and aesthetic activity, you would only succeed in substituting a worse cultural life for a better."[2]

In an order to make this point clear and concise, Lewis changed this language to the vernacular of the everyday reader in a dualist form. Lewis wrote as follows:

1. If you don't read good books, you will read bad ones;
2. If you don't go on thinking rationally, you will think irrationally; and
3. If you reject aesthetic satisfaction, you will fall into sensual satisfaction.[3]

Lewis believed that one must ultimately reject or accept the Christian story. In order to accept (or reject) the story, one should know the story. Lewis' next two missiological strategies to be covered are to be unassuming of the hearer and not to start too far along as one builds an argument.

The apologist is not to assume that the hearer knows the Christian story. For example, one should not start with the premise that the hearer really understands who Jesus is and that the Gospels are not regarded as legends. Lewis builds his argument regarding the usefulness of the two strategies quite cleverly in Chapter 19, "What Are We to Make of Jesus Christ?" in his book *God in the Dock*.

Lewis starts with three foundational implied questions about Jesus. Who is Jesus? Was he a good moral teacher? Was he a good teacher only? He showed that people who may not believe in God do like Jesus' moral teachings. Then he looks at Jesus' theological statements.

In Luke Chapter 7, a sinful woman anointed Jesus' feet with an alabaster vial of perfume at the house of one of the Pharisees. After a discussion with Simon, Jesus said, 'Therefore, I tell you, her sins, which were many, have been forgiven; hence she has shown great love...' Then he said to her, 'Your sins are forgiven' (Luke 7:47-48).

The claim to forgive sin is huge with theological implications. On the other hand, one can assert that Jesus was a lunatic. There is no evidence that Jesus was a lunatic. Moreover, Jesus was never regarded as a mere moral teacher. "He produced mainly three effects: Hatred-Terror-Adoration."[4]

One may say that Jesus' followers exaggerated the story. However, this would not make sense when the Jews believed in one God. This gives more support for the Christian story. Remember dualism, one cannot sit on the fence. One has to accept it or not. This covers the first part of this strategy, to prove the historicity and salvific power of Jesus. However, this is not enough. One may be struggling with the acceptance of Jesus because one may see the Christian story as a legend.

A good argument on the issues he cared about was important to Lewis. As a literary historian, he felt qualified to opine his view on the gospels not being a legend. His training and experience kept him from what he called personal heresy. The meaning of personal heresy is to not critique topics or concepts about which one knows little.

The avoidance of personal heresy in itself is a type of evangelistic strategy. Lewis, also along this line of thinking, fought against intentional fallacy, which is to critique an argument or literary piece solely on the name of the author.

In other words, look at the work (not the face) of an author and let that work speak for itself. Lewis wrote that the gospels are not legends. In fact, he stated that they are not artistic enough to be legends. No people writing a legend would allow most of Jesus' life to go undocumented. The gospel of John is in a class all by itself and is not parallel to any writing in ancient literature, except parts of the Platonic dialogues, according to Lewis.

In John Chapter 8 the teachers of the law and the Pharisees brought a woman caught in adultery before Jesus. They said that the Law of Moses commanded them to stone such a woman. Jesus bent down and started writing on the ground with his finger.

Lewis wrote that this episode in the Bible was inconsequential because no one has ever based a doctrine on it. Lewis stated, "And the art of inventing little irrelevant details to make an imaginary scene more convincing is a purely modern art. Surely the only explanation of this passage is that the thing really happened? The author puts it in simply because he had seen it."[5]

One must see and accept the Christian story. This story should not be watered down. In short, one must accept the supernatural to truly accept Christianity. God, the entity that made gravity, can simply suspend the law of gravity. Or God can intervene and modify the consequences of the law of gravity. The New Testament generation in the first century knew science.

C.S. Lewis was diabolically against chronological snobbery, which is an erroneous argument that people in the past were backwards because modern eyes are viewing a situation. In Matthew Chapter 1 verses 18 and 19, Jesus' mother had been engaged to Joseph but before they lived together, she was found to be with child from the Holy Spirit. Her husband Joseph, being a righteous man and unwilling to expose her to public disgrace, planned to dismiss her quietly. This proves that Joseph knew something about biology. He really believed then that Mary was impregnated by the Holy Spirit. This Holy Spirit proved to be a joy for Joseph. After the definition of joy this writer will return briefly to *The Great Divorce*.

C.S. Lewis described in *Surprised by Joy* three episodes that he experienced that left him forever seeking the same desire, which he felt briefly during these episodes.

1. The first situation was seeing a biscuit tin filled with moss.
2. The second was a glimpse at *The Tale of Squirrel Nutkin*, and
3. The third episode came through poetry.

Lewis called the desire, joy: a sensation that once experienced one wants to experience again.

This joy was not happiness or pleasure and it pointed to something beyond the episode itself. For example, if one hears beautiful music by a string instrument, Joy would not be to just hear the music again, but it would be to know who is the ultimate origin of the music. The musician or the music would be an end in itself. The music is a means to an end.

Lewis implied that if one is thirsty, then one has a need for water, a real entity. If one is hungry, one has a need for food which is real. Therefore, Lewis concluded that if one has a desire for joy, this points to a real object, a creator. This was proof that an object of joy existed which was a type of evidence that God is real.

The Great Divorce is an evangelistic book that is not addressed to the church. It is written in an unchurched language applicable to everyone. All who willing annihilate the inner idol that's keeping them from God can benefit. Lewis wrote in *The Great Divorce* and this writer concurs that, "No soul that seriously and constantly desires joy will ever miss it... To those who knock it is opened." (Lewis 2015, 75).

C.S. Lewis' missionary strategy is simple on one level, albeit profound on another. Lewis starts the book by taking a busload of souls from earth to tour the periphery of Heaven. He in effect was trying to show these souls (everyday people of various occupations) what they must do to truly knock on the door and enter Heaven. There must be an active knock to enter. This is the essential task that all men must do or what C.S. Lewis called mere Christianity.

The concept of Universalism is refuted. One has to freely make the choice and decide to enter Heaven or Hell. This is somewhat a dualist strategy. No one is exempt from this choice. The choice is simple. Actively enter Heaven or passively (by not killing the inner idol) enter Hell.

C.S. Lewis wanted to reach the outsiders. The name of one of the bright spirits in Heaven is Sarah Smith. This is a common name. It does not have the same high-powered religious impact of a Saint Monica (mother of Augustine of Hippo) or a Susanna Wesley (mother of John Wesley). Regular unchurched people would identify psychologically with this name. This is a type of vernacular that I called a psychological vernacular.

Sarah Smith, a wife and bright spirit in Heaven, is a simple name and she was a good person on earth. Although she was not known as a saint, like say Mother Teresa, she was a good person with a positive radiance. Her husband had the vice of unselfishness. Lewis' imaginative strategy is in full force with her husband, Frank.

Frank, or what is left of Frank, is described as a big ghost (tragedian) and a little ghost (dwarf). The big ghost has gotten so dominant that he has somewhat taken over the personality of Frank. The big picture is that humans can change and become part or all of their vice.

He mentioned that he gave his wife the last stamp ostensibly to fulfill a need to receive credit for this behavior. In a sharp turn, Sarah Smith apologizes to him, saying that she did not love him unselfishly. She too loved out of a craving to be loved. Now in Heaven, she is with true Love.

Lewis here is using the missiological strategy of compare and contrast to explain what real love is.

Frank also tried to attain credit because of his inner need (vice) by mentioning the day she died. Sarah displayed her glory in Heaven by not being moved by this emotional plea to fall prey to her husband's tactics. Sarah's goal of her husband to giving up his vice (knock at the door of Heaven) failed. Since he did not actively knock on this door, he, like all people who do not knock, sent himself to Hell. Lewis employs the missiological strategy of truth being better than good. The truth about salvation, Hell, and Heaven will be examined next.

Lewis may have been influenced by I Thessalonians 5:9-10. "For God has destined us not for wrath but for obtaining salvation through our Lord Jesus Christ, who died for us, so that whether we are awake or sleep we may live with him" (I Thess. 5:9-10). C.S. Lewis believed that one is saved by grace through faith. These verses argue against predestination and plainly state that man was not destined for wrath.

He did not believe like Calvinist, that man was totally depraved and played no role in his salvation. Lewis was a proponent of free will because of God's love for mankind. True liberty requires a trial. The trial is whether man will accept Jesus Christ. Jesus died for all, therefore all can accept him. The word "us" in the scriptures above represents Christians and (I believe) pre-Christians or those who at some point answer God's whisper to the soul which prevents entry into Hell.

Why did God make Hell? According to Matthew Chapter 26, verse 41, Hell was prepared for the devil and his angels. So, the question becomes: How can humankind end in Hell if it was not prepared for them? The short answer is that man becomes inhuman by continually ignoring the will of God to put him first in all things.

The human transformation concept is throughout *The Great Divorce*. One example from Chapter 9 is about a lady who grumbled continuously. One can do an act so often that one can lose objectivity and become the activity that they do. Hence, this grumbling lady (human) may have become a grumbler and more specifically ashes (non-human). If there was some life (humanity) left in the ashes, then there is hope. If this grumbler is one hundred percent ashes, then there is no hope and only Hell.

The rhetorical colluded strategy is used by the fact that Lewis is arguing against some post enlightenment thinkers that Hell is a state of mind. It is chronological snobbery to view Hell as a state of mind. In summary, Lewis is saying Hell is real whether one believes it or not. Additionally, one has the power through free will to knock on the door and be accepted to Heaven on God's terms or fall into Hell.

We saw how humans are transformed in *The Great Divorce* towards Hell. Let's look at some ways humans can be transformed through the Lord's Supper. More broadly,

Clemmie Palmer, III, MD

what is going on during Holy Communion? Should it be restricted, etc.?

Endnotes - Chapter IX: Evangelism

1. C. S. Lewis, God in the Dock (Grand Rapids: Wm. B. Eerdmans Publishing Co., 2014), 41.
2. C.S. Lewis, The Weight of Glory and Other Addresses (San Francisco: Harper One, 2001), 52.
3. C.S. Lewis, The Weight of Glory and Other Addresses (San Francisco: Harper One, 2001), 52.
4. C. S. Lewis, God in the Dock (Grand Rapids: Wm. B. Eerdmans Publishing Co., 2014), 168.
5. C. S. Lewis, God in the Dock (Grand Rapids: Wm. B. Eerdmans Publishing Co., 2014), 169.

Clemmie Palmer, III, MD

Chapter X: The Lord's Supper

The testimony of John, the disciple whom Jesus loved, makes it clear that Jesus was the Son of God and that he came with a purpose. Jews sent priests and Levites from Jerusalem to question John the Baptist since he was testifying about the Light. "'I baptized with water, but among you stands One whom you do not know'... The next day he (John the Baptist) saw Jesus coming to him and said, 'Behold, the lamb of God who takes away the sin of the world'" (John 1:26-29).

Before Jesus died for humankind's sins, he instituted the Lord's Supper and its meaning at the Last Supper by the words, "Do this in remembrance of me." This is a meal of liberation. In contrast to the Israelites, the Christian community (all who willingly accept Christ) is liberated from the bondage of sin as opposed to physical slavery in Egypt. The ritual of the Lord's Supper, just like the Passover ritual, impacts memory and therefore the culture of the people.

Moreover, the Lord's Supper strengthens the body of Christ through unity, and therefore this supper should be open to all as Jesus died for all. The Lord's Supper defends the faith against other religions, acts as a protection for Christians and helps spread the gospel. Paul's point in I Corinthian Chapter 11, which will be discussed later, was not that the Corinthians needed table manners, but they were not celebrating the Lord's Supper in accordance with the non-hierarchal and unifying Jesus in the Gospels.

The writer of this book will include several verses from Luke for completeness in that it includes the word Passover, which seemingly links this meal to the Old Testament Passover meal. "When the hour came, he took his place at the table, and the apostles with him. He said to them, 'I have eagerly desired to eat this Passover with you before I suffer; for I tell you I will not eat it until it is fulfilled in the kingdom of God.'

Then he took a cup, and after giving thanks, he said, 'Take this and divide it among yourselves; for I tell you that from now on I will not drink of the fruit of the vine until the kingdom of God comes.' Then he took a loaf of bread, and when he had given thanks, he broke it and gave it to them, saying, 'This is my body, which is given for you. Do this in remembrance of me.' And he did the same with the cup after supper, saying 'This cup that is poured out for you is the new covenant in my blood…'" (Luke 22:14-21).

In contrast, the Gospel of John and the Apostle Paul do not identify this meal as a Passover meal. However, the fact that all four Gospels placed Jesus' last supper within the season of the Passover highlights the importance of the Jewish festival upon which the meal should be understood.[1]

The Lord's Supper underwent a significant number of changes in the first centuries of the history of Christianity. A simple meal became an elaborate liturgy. Symbolically, the meaning changed from participating in the death and resurrection of Christ to a sacrifice.[2]

1. Many Christians believe that the Lord's Supper is an ancient and commonly used term which is not the case.[3] A few examples will be listed to make the point that there was much contention in the early church regarding the meal which includes but was not limited to: The name of the meal,
2. The frequency of the meal, and last, but not least,
3. The meaning of the meal.

This meal is referred to as the Lord's Supper (I Cor. 11; 20), the Lord's Table (I Cor. 10:21), an implied Communion (I Cor. 10:16), and a Thanksgiving (Eucharist) (I Corinthian 11:24). The frequency of the meal changed also. The early church dined daily (Acts 2:46), the subsequent church dined weekly (Acts 20:7), and in I Corinthians 11:26, Paul said. "For as often as you eat this bread and drink the cup, you proclaim the Lord's death until he comes."

Although there were differences in how Christians performed the Lord's Supper, most early Christians believed that Christ's Spirit was certainly present during Communion, which protected them from the adversary and by Jesus' presence they became one body in the Spirit.[4]

Christ's spiritual presence during communion changed to a real bodily presence largely as a response to a Gnostic threat. Gnostics were extreme spiritualists that believed matter was evil. Gnostics denied the humanity of Jesus. To the Gnostic, Jesus only seemed to be human. Church leaders like Ignatius responded with a materialist view of the Lord's Supper. Justin Martyr in the second century explained in his

Apology for Christianity that Christians believe that the elements of bread and wine were transmuted into Jesus' body after the food was blessed by the prayer of Jesus' words which nourishes Christians. This action is no different than Christ becoming flesh by the Word of God.[5] "The sacramental understanding of the Lord's Supper reflected in the doctrine of Christ's real presence lent itself nicely to the Church's missionary endeavors.

Christianity's main competitors from the second century on, the oriental Mystery Religions, used similar rites and observances. Most of them had fellowship meals of some sort in which it was believed that the initiated communed with one another and with their deity and even that they feasted on the body of the mystical god, thus sharing in his power over death."[6]

The rise of scholastic theology in the thirteenth century urged the church to define what a real presence of Jesus meant. Scholasticism meant theology of the schools was taught by university professors like Thomas Aquinas instead of bishops and or monks. Hildebert of Tours was the first to use the term "transubstantiation" to affirm that the bread and wine changed even though their appearance did not.

This inspired several theologians (Thomas Aquinas, Martin Luther, Huldrich Zwingli, and John Calvin) to weigh in, all from their unique perspective.[7] The concept of transubstantiation caused fear and words like superstition, and magic became correlated with the Lord's Supper which caused some worshipers to limit their participation.[8]

Nevertheless, the Lord's Supper was instituted by Jesus and serves a purpose. Who should partake of communion? What happens during communion?

According to I Corinthians 11:33, believers should partake of communion. Paul said, "My brothers and sisters, when you come together to eat, wait for one another." This verse does not exclude non-believers. Paul is merely addressing a group of believers. In other words, it would not make sense for Paul to address this Church as nonbelievers.

It is also written in I Corinthians that those who examine themselves can partake of the meal. Paul said, "Whoever, therefore, eats the bread or drinks the cup of the Lord in an unworthy manner will be answerable for the body and blood of the Lord. Examine yourselves, and only then eat of the bread and drink the cup" (I Cor. 11:27-28).

The word *unworthy* is key in the previous verses. It is this writer's view that Paul was referring to imbedded social sins of a hierarchical system that were not, for the most part, obvious to the Corinthians at the time. This writer thinks that most denominational invitations to the Lord's supper refer to conscious and overt sins that are not socially acceptable such as the violations of the ten commandments. The sins at Corinth were socially acceptable, albeit did not represent Jesus' values of humility and love.

There were divisions in the Corinthian church. Some scholars write that 1 Corinthian Chapter 11 is about wealthy Corinthians who had private meals before communion and getting larger portions during communion because of their higher rank. Other scholars believe that the divisions were based on the honor/shame code of the Mediterranean region.[9]

There were associations all over Corinth. These associations selected who could join and therefore partake of the banquets (meals). These banquets were a chief means of distributing honor which provided a social identity for its members. Additionally, there was opportunity for achieving honor in individual house churches as well. Members achieve status through their individual church roles, which Paul deplored. Whatever the main reason for the division, at Corinth, one thing is for sure; division based on economic or social structure was not the gospel.

What happens during the Lord's Supper will never be fully known. Much of what happens maybe unconscious. Certainly, remembrance of Jesus' life, death, and resurrection promotes identity for the Christian, which is passed on from generation to generation. Some believe (like Catholics) that grace is infused to believers by Jesus Christ. Others (like Baptists, Anabaptists, and Quakers) believe that the Lord's Supper, as an ordinance, serves to witness their faith. A third group believes that the Lord's Supper is nothing more than a placebo whereby partakers feel as though they have received grace from the Lord.

This writer of this book opines that there is a positive benefit from this type of placebo. One does not have to call the Lord's Supper a sacrament, but one needs to understand that there is value in partaking of the Lord's Supper. Preachers who do not wholeheartedly believe in the grace benefits of the Lord's Supper do not begin Communion by saying, "This is only an ordinance and we do not expect to receive any grace." There is a symbolic meaning of the Lord's Supper.[10]

If there is value and meaning by participating in the Lord's Supper, then it should be open to all. Why "limit" what God may or can do at the table? Therefore, all should be welcome to the Lord's Supper and henceforth nourished. Is not this the Gospel?

The Apostle Paul wrote it best: "The cup of blessing that we bless, is it not a sharing in the blood of Christ? The bread that we break, is it not a sharing in the body of Christ? Because there is one bread, we who are many are one body, for we all partake of the one bread" (I Cor. 10:16-17).

The church is the essential medium by which the impressions of Jesus' life, death, and resurrection are conveyed in time, and the Lord's Supper is a means whereby the fellowship of humankind with each other and with Christ is nourished. Therefore, all should eat at the table of unity, identity, and liberation.

Further, it would be appropriate to hear a minister retort, "If you want eternal life, please come share in the life, death, and resurrection of Jesus Christ. Don't bring your checkbook, don't bring cash. Bring an open heart and allow

Jesus to work in you. Come eat and drink. Let us all celebrate what Christ has done and what he is doing for us today.
Come and allow God's redeeming love to dwell in you. You don't have to be a member of this church. You don't have to be part of any Christian body. You do not have to be fully committed to Jesus, identified with his people, baptized, or dedicated to his cause. I am sure that there may be some doubt about whether you should come to the open table.

Doubt is not uncommon. There may have been some doubt when Jesus was at the Sea of Galilee, but the Bible says He fed 5,000 with five pieces of bread and two fish. They were satisfied. Come and see if he will satisfy you today. Everyone is invited."

Is everyone truly invited? The unclean, the non-Christian, the homosexual. I would like to turn to a fictional dialogue among three great thinkers in the field of ethics.

Endnotes - Chapter X: The Lord's Supper

1. Ronald Byars, The Sacraments in Biblical Perspective (Louisville: Westminster John Knox Press, 2011), 199.
2. E. Glenn Hinson, "The Lord's Supper in Early Church History," Review and Expositor 66, no. 1 (Winter 1969): 15.
3. Andrew McGowan, "The Myth of the 'Lord's Supper': Paul's Eucharistic Meal Terminology and Its Ancient Reception," The Catholic Biblical Quarterly 77, no. 3 (2015): 505.
4. E. Glenn Hinson, "The Lord's Supper in Early Church History," Review and Expositor 66, no. 1 (Winter 1969): 20.
5. E. Glenn Hinson, "The Lord's Supper in Early Church History," Review and Expositor 66, no. 1 (Winter 1969): 20.
6. E. Glenn Hinson, "The Lord's Supper in Early Church History," Review and Expositor 66, no. 1 (Winter 1969): 23.
7. Ronald Byars, The Sacraments in Biblical Perspective (Louisville: Westminster John Knox Press, 2011), 242.
8. Donald Hustad, "The Lord's Supper for Baptists: A Spiritual Meal, a Snack, or a Placebo?" Review and Expositor 106, no. 2 (Spring 2009): 176.
9. Rachel McRae, "Eating with Honor: The Corinthian Lord's Supper in Light of Voluntary Association Meal Practices," Journal of Biblical Literature 130, no. 1 (2011): 167-168.

10. Donald Hustad, "The Lord's Supper for Baptists: A Spiritual Meal, a Snack, or a Placebo?" Review and Expositor 106, no. 2 (Spring 2009): 180-181.

Chapter XI: Homosexuality and the Church

Dialogue

Don Chandler: Thank you all for being concerned about Shepherd Presbyterian Church by responding to the More Light churches' call for information and advice regarding a resolution presented by our Social Involvement Committee. I understand that you all have some of the best minds in the field of homosexuality and the church. For the record, I want to say that James Packer, John Boswell, and Eugene Rogers are not financially benefiting from this forum.

My pastor, Elaine Campbell, wants me to take the lead on this issue and lobby the congregation in a manner which would be uplifting to the church. I, therefore, need your assistance so that an informed decision can be made. This discussion will last no more than one hour or until I have decided on the resolution, whichever comes first. All of you have read the comments that several church members have made to me about their concerns regarding the ordination and election of homosexuals as church leaders. Packer, will you start us off?"

Packer:	[Smiling] I don't know why you choose me first, but I will do the best I can to make sure you are informed on the Word as I understand it. First, it should be emphasized that your national governing body has ruled to exclude homosexual members for election and ordination as church leaders. This should, in and of itself, settle any matter that the church may have. We all have rules. There is a speed limit for drivers, a law for the Hebrew people, and a church body to rule on ecclesial disputes.
Rogers:	[Interrupting...] I see where this is going. The national governing body is not God. That 1978 ruling is antiquated, discriminatory, and may have been homophobic.
Boswell:	That Judicial ruling may be the only thing that the church has to 'legally' discriminate against homosexuals. One sure can't find a bona fide reason to discriminate in scripture.
Don Chandler:	[Thinking... I need to listen because I have to face a 130--member, well educated, mostly young congregation who has an interest in social ministry.]
Packer:	[Thinking, I need to influence Don Chandler and counterattack Boswell.] No disrespect Boswell, but I can't believe what you just uttered. Patty Becker, a member of Shepherd Church said, and I

	agree, that the Bible calls homosexuality a sin.
Boswell:	The word homosexual wasn't coined until the late nineteenth century. It wasn't in the original Bible.[1]
Packer:	The word Trinity isn't in the original Hebrew Bible nor in any current Bibles either, but we agree on the concept. Therefore, just because the word homosexual was not in the original Bible does not mean we can't agree that it is a sin.
Rogers:	Whether or not the word homosexual is in the Bible is irrelevant to our Christian duty to properly interpret scripture.
Boswell:	Let me add to Rogers. We need to interpret scripture outside of our social location.
Rogers:	I vehemently agree with that comment.
Packer:	Theoretically, one may be able to interpret scripture outside of our social location, albeit it would be difficult. Rogers are you a liberal theologian?
Rogers:	Yes.
Packer:	Liberation theology, in my opinion, is all about social location. Can you present an example whereby a scripture can be interpreted outside of social location?
Rogers:	Alberto Tarver, church member, attacked the More Light resolution by implying that Paul classified homosexuality with idolatry.

Boswell: That's a good point Rogers but not as strong as a real discussion on the account of Sodom in Genesis Chapter 19.

Rogers: I thought about introducing that topic, but didn't want to get into the issue of homosexual rape along with a lack of hospitality which I think were the two issues that led to the destruction of Sodom. Plus, Boswell, you are the guru on Sodom.

Boswell: [Smiling] I'm not sure if that's a compliment or not. As you may know, Sodom is a symbol of evil (and not homosexuality) in the Bible.[2]

The entire forum laughed briefly.

Packer: Gentlemen, let's get back to the topic of social location. Alberto Tarver was right by asserting that Paul classified homosexuality with idolatry.

Rogers: This is misleading. Paul was not attacking homosexuals in Romans Chapter 1.

Packer: Who was Paul attacking then? From my memory, I believe that Paul wrote that women exchanged the natural function for that which is unnatural, and men abandoned the natural function of the woman (Romans 1:26-27).

Rogers: Paul lists many types of people in Romans Chapter 1: slanderers, haters of God, and the arrogant. He was building an argument.

Packer:	[After a sigh, not wanting to sound arrogant.] Nevertheless, homosexuals are still in the list here. Do you agree with that Rogers?
Rogers:	[Thinking to himself, Packer is not letting up off the gas… I know what I am saying is right. I think that I'll ask for a bathroom break to gather my thoughts and calm down. He is looking directly in my eyes.] I think that I need a…
Boswell:	[Interrupting Rogers] I got you Rogers.
Rogers:	[Thinking, that's a relief] Thank you.
Boswell:	Idolatry is the focus of Paul's argument in Romans Chapter one, not gays and lesbians.
Packer:	Boswell, you are a systematic thinker with excellent credentials. In short, you are a true scholar. Can you explain your interpretation of Paul's focus in the first Chapter of Romans?"
Boswell:	Thank you. There is nothing in the context of the scriptures in Romans Chapter one that supports the opinion that Paul condemned homosexuality. Paul was talking to a heterosexual Gentile audience. These verses wouldn't make sense if Paul was talking to a homosexual group. Paul chose as an illustration the sin of idolatry, which he knew would resonate to the Jews. The Jews, while reading these scriptures would be saying, 'tell them like it is Paul.'

	Then Paul dropped the rhetorical bombshell when he declares that Jewish idolatry in Romans 2:1 is just as sinful as Gentile idolatry and therefore all is guilty in Romans 3:23."
Packer:	[Interrupting and trying to break Boswell train of thought] The fact that Jews worshiped false gods involving same sex rituals in Leviticus doesn't really help your argument. Moreover, it is clearly written in Leviticus 18:22 that homosexuality is an abomination.
Boswell:	Packer, we are getting off topic here. I was trying to explain Paul's illustration. I would just say that the word abomination was derived from the Hebrew word toevah, which signifies something ritually unclean, not sin. Back to Romans Chapter one. Paul's point was that all are sinners. The idolatry of the Gentiles who worshiped false gods was the same as the idolatry of the Jews worshiping false Gentile gods in the Old Testament.
Packer:	I understand your point. But as a Calvinist, I think that humankind should engage in appropriate, marital, and non-skewed sex in order to glorify God.
Rogers:	Packer, are you saying that homosexuals are skewed statistically as compared to heterosexuals? Or, are you saying that homosexuals are freaks of nature?

Packer:	[Thinking, if I say nature that would lead us down the road of natural law - Shepherd Presbyterian church has probably moved beyond natural law theory - and I would sound insensitive since he used the word freak, but if I say statistically then modern science may contradict me... I am going to reintroduce the Apostle Paul and try to imply the natural law tradition.] Well, as I stated earlier, Paul wrote that women exchanged the natural function for that which is unnatural, and men abandoned the natural function of the woman (Romans 1:26-27). I believe that Paul and Thomas Aquinas were on the same page on this issue.
Boswell:	[Grimacing] That's a good one Packer. I do not believe Paul was thinking of natural law in Romans Chapter one. Aquinas didn't fully complete his natural law work until at least a millennium after Paul's writings.
Packer:	"Paul definitely used the word natural. Mankind should know by reasoning the behavior required to guide human existence (procreate, social structure, etc.)."
Boswell:	For Paul, nature was equivalent to character. It had nothing to do with universal law or moral truth. If Uncle Bob's disposition is pleasant, one may say he is good by nature. On the other hand, if Uncle Bob's

	disposition is unpleasant, one may say that he has an evil nature.
Packer:	Ok, I see your point, Boswell. Can an evil nature please God?

Silence in the room.

Don Chandler:	[Texted Pastor Campbell It is so quiet in the room that a mouse could be heard urinating on cotton.]
Rogers:	According to Dennis Bench, an outspoken member of Shepherd Presbyterian church, that we are all one in Christ Jesus and heirs of the promise of God.
Packer:	Wait a minute, some are predestined to be saved, but not all.
Boswell:	Remember John 3:16, 2 Corinthians 5:15, and 1 Timothy 4:10 among other scriptures.
Rogers:	Homosexuals are church members and partakers of the Eucharist. Sacraments are outward signs that signify the grace they confer. Therefore, the grace of salvation is given to homosexuals too through the Eucharist.[3] Full members of the church (the body of Christ) who have the right to the Eucharist should be eligible for election and ordination as church leaders.
Don Chandler:	I have heard the arguments from all the scholars and would like to thank the members of this forum for participating. I will call Pastor Campbell and tell her

> whether or not I support homosexuals taking communion or their ordination as church leaders.

Don Chandler's recommendation will be based on several factors, which include but are not limited to:

1. A discriminatory 1978 ruling,
2. The word homosexual wasn't in the original bible,
3. Sodom is a symbol of evil, not homosexuality,
4. Paul in Romans Chapter 1 was not attacking homosexuals but idolatry, and was not referring to natural law tradition.
5. The Levitical codes were about uncleanness, not sin,
6. Natural law doesn't adequately explain human sexuality, and
7. Jesus died for all.

However, Don Chandler was not willing to tell the panel his decision.

Again, I write, and you decide.

Everyone learns in a different way. It is important to really grasp the concept of forgiveness is throughout the Bible. Some people really like dialogues, some like lectures, and others like sermons, etc.

Next is a short sermon that should help cement what God inspired on forgiveness. This sermon is written just as it was delivered.

Endnotes - Chapter XI: Homosexuality & the Church

1. John Boswell, "Homosexuality in the Scriptures," in Christian Ethics: An Introductory Reader, ed. Samuel Wells (Malden: Wiley-Blackwell, 2010), 262-264.
2. John Boswell, "Homosexuality in the Scriptures," in Christian Ethics: An Introductory Reader, ed. Samuel Wells (Malden: Wiley-Blackwell, 2010), 262-264.
3. Eugene Rogers, "Sanctification, Homosexuality, and God's Triune Life," in Christian Ethics: An Introductory Reader, ed. Samuel Wells (Malden: Wiley-Blackwell, 2010), 265-267.

Chapter XII: Sermon on Forgiveness

Text: Mark 16:1-8
Sermon Title: A Deep Moment of Despair
Focus: We all have denied Jesus at some point in our life, but we can be forgiven.
Function: Mankind needs to know that we serve a second chance God.
Bad News, Text: Peter did not keep a vow to Jesus and suffered from despair.
Bad News, Our World: There is a big price to pay when Jesus is denied.
Good News, Text: Jesus keeps his promises.
Good News, Our World: Jesus overlooks our denials and forgives us through grace.
Key Concretizations: After Jesus' resurrection, he told Peter to follow him, which implied forgiveness.
A Deep Moment of Despair
Good Morning Church
To those of you who have hope in your life and to those of you who have little or no hope, I greet you in the name of Jesus the Christ.
Prayer:
Lord, I pray that I present a message that will touch someone today, that will lead them out of the darkness of despair. Hide me behind the cross… So that you will get the glory you deserve. In Jesus' name, I pray, amen.

Topic: A deep moment of despair.

Mark 16:1-8 (The Resurrection of Jesus)

1. When the Sabbath was over, Mary Magdalene, and Mary the mother of James, and Salome bought spices so that they might go and anoint him.
2. And very early on the first day of the week, when the sun had risen, they went to the tomb.
3. They had been saying to one another, "Who will roll away the stone for us from the entrance to the tomb?"
4. When they looked up, they saw that the stone, which was very large, had already been rolled back.
5. As they entered the tomb, they saw a young man, dressed in a white robe, sitting on the right side; and they were alarmed.
6. But he said to them, "Do not be alarmed; you are looking for Jesus of Nazareth, who was crucified. He has been raised; he is not here. Look, there is the place they laid him.
7. But go, tell his disciples and Peter that he is going ahead of you to Galilee; there you will see him, just as he told you."
8. So they went out and fled from the tomb, for terror and amazement had seized them; and they said nothing to anyone, for they were afraid. (Jewish law, which was very male dominated, discounted the witness of women.[1])

Church good news cannot be contained. After they composed themselves, they did a lot of talking (Matt 28:8; Luke 24:9).

Three Problems in Mark 16:1-8
   1. Jesus was killed during the Sabbath. Jewish rules forbade handling dead bodies during the Sabbath. His

friends and family couldn't properly embalm and anoint his body. They went to the tomb later to find the greatest surprise of their lives.
2. Unbelief.
3. Implicit denial and forgiveness of Peter and the other disciples.

There was unbelief during the early morning walk to the tomb by the three women. They went to do the work of undertakers (concerned about the stone at the tomb). There was no need to worry. The stone was already rolled away. Not to let Jesus out, but to let them go in. Unbelief is fertile ground to worry.

*Focus on verse 6 and 7.
In verse 6, they were commissioned by an angel to not be alarmed.

Verse 6. "Do not be alarmed."
(But he said to them, "Do not be alarmed; you are looking for Jesus of Nazareth, who was crucified. He has been raised; he is not here. Look, there is the place they laid him.)

*This is a present imperative with a negative particle, which usually means to stop an act already in progress. Humans are always awed and frightened at the physical manifestation of the spiritual realm.[2]

Verse 7. "But go, tell his disciples and Peter that he is going ahead of you to Galilee; there you will see him, just as he told you."

The verb translated "is going ahead" could mean to precede or to lead. Both make sense in this context, but the former is to be preferred because of the statement "There you will see him."[3] This alludes to the promise in Mark 14:28 (Reference to Galilee)

These men needed reassurance and encouragement during this dark time. Why Galilee?

Remember, the place where Jesus gives last minute instructions before his ascension.
   a. This is the place where they were originally called. (A new beginning)
   b. Or Mark used traditions from Galilean communities.
   c. Or this is what I refer to as a promise which was made in Mark 14:28.

"And Jesus said to them as they went, 'You will all become deserters; for it is written, I will strike the shepherd, and the sheep will be scattered. But after I am raised up, I will go before you to Galilee'" (Mark 14:27-30).

"Peter said to him, 'Even though all become deserters, I will not.'

Jesus said to him, 'Truly I tell you, this day, this very night, before the cock crows twice, you will deny me three times.'"

After Peter's denial... he remembered this conversation and broke down and wept (Mark 14:72).

God, the World, and Me

*Oh, I wish that I can meet my brother, Peter.

There are some other people in the first century that I would like to meet Lazarus, the Gerasene Demoniac, the lady with the issue of blood and the blind beggar by the roadside.

*What was your relationship with Jesus like, Peter?
What did Jesus talk about at dinner?
Did he have an interest in sports?
How did he deal with people talking about him...? (Scribes, Pharisees, and the priests)

*Why Peter? Mark 16:7 ***Unique relationship
1. Peter's mother-in-law was in bed with a fever and Jesus took her by the hand and the fever left her (Mark 1:29).
2. Peter (James & John) was there when Jesus said "Talitha cum" (little girl get up) to a dead girl and immediately she got up and began to walk (Mark 5:4).
3. Who walked on water (Matthew 14:28-31).
4. It was Peter who made the great confession.
You are the Messiah (Mark 8:29).
5. It was Peter who rebuked Jesus after Jesus told his disciples that he will undergo great suffering, be killed and in three days rise again.
6. It was Peter along with James & John, who saw Jesus' transfiguration (Elijah & Moses).
Only Peter asks, Rabbi is it good for us to be here (Mark 9:4-5).
7. It was Peter who was called by name in Gethsemane.
Simone are you asleep? Could you not keep awake one hour?

Keep awake and pray that you do not come into the time of trial; the spirit is indeed willing, but the flesh is weak (Mark 14:37-38).

8. At the arrest of Jesus, it was Peter (John 18:10) who cut off the right ear of the high priest's slave. Jesus asked, "Am I not to drink the cup that the father has given me?"
9. It was Peter who was instructed on forgiveness.
"'Lord, if another member of the church sins against me, how often should I forgive? As many as seven times?'
Jesus said to him, 'Not seven times, but I tell you, seventy times seven'" (Matthew 18:21-22).

Peter needs to know that he was not forsaken.
Some scholars say that Peter's superiority had ceased for a time and it had to be restored.[4]
Nevertheless, when Jesus decides he is going to use you, he is going to use you.
Jesus had already made up his mind (Mark 14:28) that he was going to forgive his disciples who all fell away.

Peter vowed never to leave Jesus…
Just like Peter, we make vows that we break.

Personally, I have
    1. Said things that I shouldn't have said,
    2. Gone places that I shouldn't have gone, and
    3. Have done things that I shouldn't have done.
I am thankful that the Lord is a forgiving God.
Peter needed to know that he had been forgiven.
"But after I am raised up, I will go before you in Galilee" (Mark 14:28).

God, the World, and Me

Remember, Peter followed Jesus at a distance. (He was no coward.)
He mingled with the enemies of Jesus. (Just like we do.)
He warmed himself by the fire. (Suggest the wrong fire.)
He denied Jesus three times.
But was forgiven (John Chapter 21 & Mark 16:7)
You can be forgiven too.
In John Chapter 21, Jesus asked Peter three times if he loved him. (What a correlation to the three denials)
End result, Jesus said, "Follow me."

Peter no longer felt disqualified.
To fail does not make one a lifelong failure.
The cross and the resurrection reach out to all.

I hope this offers you comfort in your moments of despair.

Let the church say Amen.

Endnotes - Chapter XII: Sermon on Forgiveness

1. Rodney Cooper, Mark, vol. 2, Holman New Testament Commentary (Nashville, TN: Broadman & Holman Publishers, 2000), 275-276.
2. Robert Utley, The Gospel According to Peter: Marl and I & II Peter, Volume 2, Study Guide Commentary Series (Marshall, Texas: Bible Lessons International, 2000), 200-2053.
3. James Brooks, Mark, vol. 23, The New American Commentary (Nashville: Broadman & Holman Publishers, 1991), 271.
4. John Peter Lange, Philip Schaff, and William G. T. Shedd, A Commentary on the Holy Scriptures: Mark (Bellingham, WA: Logos Bible Software, 2008), 157.

A Personal Note from the Author

It is my hope that the reader will research at least one reference contained herein and see the Bible in a new light, opening the door to an illuminating and life-changing experience. This exercise may lead to a greater appreciation of God's grace.

Then I would love for all readers to say, "Lord, thank you for my brain that I may know you, and for my heart that I can love you."

Clemmie Palmer, III, MD

About the Author

Clemmie Palmer, III, MD is a psychiatrist who practices primarily in Alabama. In addition, he also does telepsychiatry in California, Florida, and Georgia.

Education and Publications:

He earned a bachelor's degree in Physical Science in 1989 from Auburn University – Montgomery and a medical degree from the University of Alabama in 1994. He completed a residency in general psychiatry in 1998.

He wrote a chapter on "Cyclothymic Disorder" in *Current Psychiatric Diagnosis & Treatment*, copyright 1999 and is the author of God, the World, and Me, copyright 2018.

Clemmie's years of clinical work led him to pursue a theological education. He graduated Magna Cum Laude from Hood Theological Seminary in 2016.

Family: Clemmie is married to Veronica and has two children, Clemmie IV and Angel. He resides in Montgomery, Alabama.

Personal: In his spare time, Clemmie enjoys jazz and blues, traveling, playing chess and reading theology.

www.ingramcontent.com/pod-product-compliance
Lightning Source LLC
Chambersburg PA
CBHW050639160426
43194CB00010B/1728